Topeka and Santa Fé railway co. Atchison

Texas coast country

Briefly describing the resources of counties along the Gulf, Colorado &

Santa Fé railway line

Topeka and Santa Fé railway co. Atchison

Texas coast country
Briefly describing the resources of counties along the Gulf, Colorado & Santa Fé railway line

ISBN/EAN: 9783337238766

Printed in Europe, USA, Canada, Australia, Japan

Cover: Foto ©Andreas Hilbeck / pixelio.de

More available books at **www.hansebooks.com**

IN A STRAWBERRY FIELD.

Texas Coast Country

* * *

Also briefly describing
the resources of
Counties along the
Gulf, Colorado & Santa Fe
Railway line

* * *

120TH THOUSAND

Issued by the Passenger Department
Santa Fe Route
October, 1899.

Corbitt & Butterfield Co.,
Railway Printers,
Chicago.

Somewhat Personal

..

DO you live in a climate where the winters are long and severe? In Texas there is practically no winter; one can comfortably work outdoors the year round.

Is your locality subject to devastating drouths? In the Coast Country of Texas the average rainfall is fifty inches a year, well distributed through the growing season; and no irrigation is required.

Is the soil of your farm worn out? Texas soil rarely requires fertilizers; it is deep and rich and permanent.

Does it require all you earn for living expenses? The cost is 40% less to build a house in Texas than in the North, 50% less for clothing, and 80% less for fuel.

Are you now restricted to one main crop a year? Along the Gulf Coast of Texas a man can raise two or three crops of vegetables and alfalfa per annum, and more than one crop of some other staples; a great diversity is also possible.

Are you interested in horticulture? Texas fruit lands annually pay $200 to $500 net per acre. The fruit season begins early and lasts to a late date.

Is your northern farm worth $100 an acre, with a high tax rate and low prices for products? Why not try the $10 an acre lands in the southern part of Texas, where taxes are low and markets excellent?

This pamphlet is intended for the man desirous of more information on the important subject of where to go for a new home. The descriptions are limited to the southern portion of Texas, along the Gulf

Coast, with some information about other sections on the Gulf, Colorado & Santa Fe Railway. Farmers, fruit-raisers, land-owners and real estate agents are permitted to speak for themselves. The unsigned articles have been compiled from the most reliable sources.

Here is a country which it is believed offers ample rewards for well-directed toil; where the homeseeker may find cheap land, abundant crops, good markets, a friendly climate and hospitable neighbors.

If, after reading what is herein contained, you are sufficiently interested to wish to investigate further by taking a trip to Texas and seeing for yourself, remember that the Santa Fe Route is the direct line from Chicago, Kansas City, Denver and other northern and eastern points to the heart of the Coast Country. For full particulars respecting train service, ticket rates, etc., confer with any ticket agent or address the undersigned.

W. J. BLACK, General Passenger Agent,
Atchison, Topeka & Santa Fe Ry.,
TOPEKA, KANSAS.

C. A. HIGGINS, Ass't Gen'l Passenger Agent,
Atchison, Topeka & Santa Fe Ry.,
CHICAGO.

W. S. KEENAN, General Passenger Agent,
Gulf, Colorado & Santa Fe Ry.,
GALVESTON, TEXAS.

facts About Texas

• • •

Historical The fascinating story of Texas' early life began, so far as white occupation is concerned, with La Salle's visit to Matagorda Bay in 1685. Later, in 1692, European settlements were made at San Antonio, and in 1717 at Nacogdoches. Following the rout of the Mexicans at the battle of San Jacinto in 1836 a republic was declared, and in 1845 Texas came into the Union. Here on the Mexican border has been successfully evolved, by strenuous effort from diverse elements, a united and prosperous people noted for chivalric courtesy, civic pride and material greatness.

Its Rank Texas takes first prize in regard to area, production of cotton, number of sheep, cattle and horses raised; amount of funds set apart for free public schools and colleges, and the size and finish of the beautiful capitol building at Austin. It ranks fourth in wealth, about third in railroad mileage, and fifth in population.

A Comparison With only six per cent of its land cultivated, Texas produces more rice than South Carolina, more sugar and sorghum than Louisiana, and more wheat than the Dakotas. It has more prairie land than Kansas, a larger coal area than Pennsylvania, and greater oak forests than West Virginia; it raises more cotton than Mississippi; can produce more iron ore than Alabama, and excels New Hampshire in granite.

The State debt is less than $4,000,000. Taxable valuation is about $900,000,000. Legal rate of interest is 6 per cent, but 10 per cent may be charged. These figures compare favorably with eastern commonwealths.

Its Area The Lone Star State extends from the 26th to the 36th parallel of latitude and lies between the 94th and 106th degrees of longitude. The average length, east and west, is 800 miles, and average breadth, north and south, 750 miles. It possesses 400 miles of coast line; has navigable rivers equaling those of any five other states, and 8,952 miles of railroad, mostly trunk lines. From Texarkana to El Paso equals the distance from New York to Chicago. A man bicycling on its boundary lines would travel over 4,000 miles. There are 262,290 square miles of "room," and hardly thirteen people yet to each square mile. The Austrian empire, with about the same area, sustains a population of 36,000,000; the German empire, with less area has more than 50,000,000 inhabitants. Texas could sustain a population of 95,000,000 within a territory equal to that of the British Isles, Denmark, Greece, Holland, Switzerland, Turkey and Belgium. A recent census shows that 255,000 farmers cultivate their own land, 95,000 are tenants and 56,000 day laborers.

A VOYAGE DOWN CHOCOLATE BAYOU

Topography Beginning with a level coast, there is a gradual ascent north and west, to an elevation of 4,000 feet, which affords excellent drainage. Three-fourths of this vast area can be profitably cultivated. The southeastern and southern sections are level and free from rock—here is the famous fruit belt, rivaling California. Dense forests of red and live oak, cedar, blackjack, mesquite, hackberry, sweet gum, pecan, walnut, cottonwood, sycamore, cypress, ash, elm, hickory and pine cover the eastern district—there being 25,000,000 acres of merchantable pine alone. The timber lands comprise 45,000,000 acres, with 67,500,000,000 feet of standing timber. The center of Texas is an undulating prairie, like the prolific plains of Kansas, with succulent grasses—a fine stock country and capable of raising immense crops of corn, wheat and cotton. West Texas is broken by hills and mountains, with fertile valleys. The Panhandle region is a table-land, and noted for its fat cattle.

Soils As a rule the rich, deep soil of Texas needs no fertilizer for standard crops. A moderate top-dressing of cotton-seed helps to make a larger crop, but is not absolutely required. Anything can be raised that grows in the temperate zone. Sugar cane, cotton, figs, olives, pears and grapes are a remarkable success in the South. The Mediterranean countries do not excel the Texas Coast Country in raising fruit. In the Western sections the rainfall is sometimes insufficient, but artesian wells and irrigation are aiding the agriculturist to control the water supply. As a general thing plenty of rain falls throughout other sections to mature crops.

Texas furnishes its citizens a good living.

Products In 1895 the various products of this State (from fields, gardens, orchards, ranches and factories) amounted to $223,000,000. The values of the leading crops were: cotton and cotton seed, $61,000,000; corn, $29,000,000; wheat, $7,500,000; oats, $5,400,000; garden produce, $2,850,000; potatoes, $2,705,000; hay, $1,335,000; sugar cane, molasses and sorghum, $3,000,000; peaches, apples, grapes, plums, pears and melons, $1,645,000; millet, barley and rye, $685,000; garden crops, $2,635,000; hay, $1,140,000.

Texas ranks seventh as a corn producing state, first in sheep, eighth in hogs, and her herds of cattle are one-sixth of the entire number in the United States.

In 1897 live stock was assessed at $78,365,590, the leading items being horses and mules, cattle, sheep and hogs. Even the despised goat is quoted at a quarter of a million " simoleons."

Schools. etc. Material wealth is not all. Texas has accumulated a permanent school fund (comprising lands and securities) of $75,000,000. During 1898-99, 11,045 white and

9

2,958 colored teachers were employed in public schools, and enough more in private institutions to bring the total up to 15,000. Land Commissioner Baker reports 38,000,000 acres of land surveyed for the permanent school fund. All prominent religious denominations are well represented by thriving churches, and society in general is of the highest order. The hospitality of Texas is proverbial; the latch-string is always out.

"A LITTLE FARM, WELL TILLED."

Public Lands There still remains upwards of 4,000,000 acres of public land subject to pre-emption by three years continuous residence. By this means a married man may secure 160 acres and a single man 80 acres. The vast bodies of unsold lands belonging to the school fund are leased on favorable terms.

Resources Coal and iron are plentiful, coal being found in thirty counties; one bituminous coal formation on the Red River covers 12,000 square miles, with seams three feet in thickness. Bituminous and lignite coals are mined in the Nueces district, along the Rio Grande River. Extensive deposits of iron are reported to exist in eastern Texas, covering 1,000 square miles of surface, many veins being ten feet thick. There are surface indications of petroleum in several counties

along the eastern border, and paying wells have been
sunk at Nacogdoches. Natural gas has been discovered in several sections. Besides these three
fields of iron, three of coal and three of oil, three
distinct districts of copper have been opened up—
the ores of the Trans-Pecos region being extensively
worked. Gold and silver mines have been discovered near El Paso, and a 140-foot bed of rock salt
underlies Victoria. Salt mines are profitably worked
in a number of counties. Gypsum occurs in the
Abilene Country. Asphaltum, bat guano, marls,
mica and granite are found in paying quantities.

There is an abundance of sand-stone and marble
of finest quality and colors. The clays of Texas
are unsurpassed for making brick and pottery, while
lime and cement are easily produced.

Climate In general the climate of Texas is
pleasant and healthful. The heat of
summer is alleviated either by altitude, as at El
Paso, or sea breezes, as at Galveston, or constant
land breezes, as on the interior plains. In winter
there is very little cold weather along the Gulf, but
in north and northwest Texas an occasional
"norther" forces people indoors for a brief time.
The extremes of heat and cold are not so great as
occur farther north. Farm work may be carried on
the year round with but little interruption from
severe storms.

Letting El Paso (3,700 feet) represent the Trans-
Pecos region of Texas, Galveston (sea level) the
Gulf Coast section, while San Antonio, Austin and

THE SEALY HOSPITAL AT GALVESTON.

11

Palestine (600 feet each) stand for the Western, Central and Eastern districts respectively, and the following figures regarding temperature and rainfall will show the variations in different parts of this vast empire — mean annual rainfall — El Paso, 13.14 inches; Galveston, 52.80 inches; Austin, 35.78 inches; Palestine, 47.56 inches; San Antonio, 32.31 inches.

The mean spring, summer, autumn and winter temperatures for the same places are:

LOCATION.	Spring Degrees.	Summer Degrees.	Autumn Degrees.	Winter Degrees.
Galveston	69.8	83.6	71.4	55.3
Austin	67.7	83.3	67.7	51.8
Palestine...........	65.3	79.9	66.5	47.6
San Antonio	69.6	82.3	68.7	53.8
El Paso.............	73.6	80.5	62.3	47.3

The wealth on top of the ground, waiting to be tickled into a laughing harvest by the man with the plow, is what Texas depends upon to attract settlers. And while cotton, corn and wheat are the "standbys"—cotton leading in importance—the beautiful region on the Gulf Coast, where ten acres will support a family and twenty acres is a competence, is crowding other sections for first place.

FAMILY PETS.

12

The Coast Country

• • •

Where It Is The Coast region of Texas comprises that part of the State bordering the Gulf of Mexico, from Sabine River to the Rio Grande and extending inland nearly one hundred miles. This pamphlet is more particularly concerned with the portion immediately tributary to the line of the Santa Fe Route, embracing the counties of Harris, Galveston, Brazoria, Ft. Bend, Wharton and Jackson.

The location of the Coast country gives to it unequaled advantages and possibilities. Lying on the borders of the temperate and tropic zones, and on the northern shore of a great inland sea, the nipping and eager air of winter and the withering waves of scorching summer heat are not known. There is the gentle, budding springtime, lengthening out into the long days of June; succeeded by summer, Nature's ripening time, which the trade-winds daily sweeping northward from the Gulf temper to a delightful coolness; and then the long, bright, sunny fall, ending with a short, mild winter.

What It Is This is in general a prairie country, an undulating plain, rising five feet to the mile northward from the Gulf, and embracing large forest areas along its water courses. The timber is chiefly oak, live oak, ash, walnut, pecan, mesquite and sycamore. To the west of the Brazos River in the coast country are great tracts of cedar. For several years there has been a large export trade in cedar logs cut far in the interior, hauled to the Brazos and then shipped by boat or rail to Galveston, where they are transhipped to Europe. The general surface is sixty to one hundred feet above mean tide level, most of it sufficiently rolling to afford good drainage into numerous local streams and bayous, which in turn empty into the bays along the great Gulf. Good water for domestic uses is found everywhere under the clay . subsoil, and artesian wells are numerous. There are few localities but which can be inexpensively drained and the fertile land thus rendered fit for the plow.

Proper drainage is the main problem here—how to get rid of surplus surface water. An underlying stratum of quicksand affords almost perfect sub-irrigation.

The Soil In the river valleys the soil is a deep black, sandy loam. Fertilizers do not seem to be required. There is no "wear out" to it because formed of alluvial deposits originating in the rich lands of the North. The prairie soil consists of three kinds of sandy loam, friable and easily tilled; it rots quicker than the stiffer sod of Illinois or Kansas. It is covered with a very compact sod, that must be broken and allowed to rot before it

GUNNING FOR WILD FOWL ON BUFFALO BAYOU.

can be pulverized and, even then there seems to be something that requires air and heat to rectify before it will produce well. One year's work will bring it into good productive condition, when, with proper fertilizing, it cannot be surpassed. For pears alone this is not necessary, as experience has fully proved that if set on sod that has been simply lapped over with several turns of the plow, the trees will grow about as well as if the ground had been previously prepared.

The black waxy or hog wailow loam (suitable for sugar cane, cotton and berries), is exceedingly rich, though more difficult to till. These soils are no better than those found in the Missouri, Miami,

Scioto or Kansas valleys. Their chief value lies in the rare combination which Southern Texas offers of a rich soil, abundant rainfall and genial climate.

Cbe Rainfall The annual rainfall of the Texas coast district within the rain belt is from 43 to 65 inches, well distributed throughout the spring and summer; besides, the heavy dews, a characteristic feature of the region, furnish a source of daily refreshment for all forms of plant life.

Varied Crops Both soil and climate are adapted to the bountiful production of a greater variety of field, garden and orchard crops than any like extent of territory in the United States. Indeed, omitting the apple, it is well nigh impossible to mention any field, garden or fruit crop which may not be grown here in the greatest abundance, and of finest quality, if only the right varieties be selected.

Fruits rivaling those of California and vegetables equal to any grown in the North are ready for market here a month to six weeks earlier than in the district which has hitherto enjoyed a monopoly of supplying eastern cities. This is possible because the crop season along the Gulf Coast of Texas begins early and stays late. During one of these long periods two and three crops of many varieties of farm and garden products may be grown, and the soil apparently still be as vigorous as ever. Corn, oats, sorghum, hay, Irish potatoes, sweet potatoes, sugar cane, Egyptian and Sea Island cotton, Cuban tobacco, figs, pears, plums, grapes—the list might be expanded into a small catalogue. They all do well. The farmer and horticulturist does not have to urge forward his restless team of sun and soil. Rather they require holding back, lest the land produce too abundantly, beyond the capacity of its owner to properly care for the resultant marvelous crops.

Fish abound in all the streams, while in the waters of the Gulf they are so plentiful as to fill the local markets with a variety of finny creatures whose puzzling names sound queerly to the landsman. And oysters—they can be had for the mere trouble of gathering, if one will go to the Gulf.

The man who deliberately stays hungry and poor

in the Coast Country is worthless and lazy beyond redemption.

Lay siege to a South Texas plantation and you could not starve out the owner. He would still contentedly fill his old cob pipe with home grown tobacco, every bit as good as the imported leaf; and shake down ripe walnuts and pecans from trees in the timber lot for winter use. Luscious pears, peaches, strawberries and figs would form his dessert ten months in the year. Hardly a day would pass without fresh vegetables on the table plucked from his own truck patch. From the product of white acres of cotton and flocks of sheep could be fashioned homespun garments good enough for anybody.

ONLY TWO YEARS FROM THE SOD

Rich cane fields would contribute syrup and sugar. Fat hogs and sleek cattle would grow fatter and sleeker on river bottom corn and be transformed into bacon or beef. There is also plenty of fuel close at hand—while bayou and stream sustain fish in abundance. Even the vagrant winds bring in wild fowl from the Gulf. No one can be quite so independent as the man who owns a good farm in the Coast Country.

Cost of Land Farm and garden land in the Gulf Coast belt now costs from $10 to $25 per acre in small tracts, with a reduction if bought in large bodies. In the immediate vicinity of railroad depots and in some other-wise specially favored localities, a higher price is asked. There is considerable good fruit, berry and vegetable land, not yet taken, which can be pur-chased at an average price per acre of $10 to $15. Water rights for surface irrigation (as in California) are not necessary, because the abundant rainfall is supplemented by sub-irrigation.

Improvements Supposing the land you buy is raw prairie. The first thing required is shelter for family and stock—the next, a suitable fence. A two-room box house, set on wooden blocks or stones, with two flues, may be built for $150; for three rooms allow $225; four rooms $325. A two-room frame house, plain finish with porch will cost $325; three rooms $480; four rooms $640, and five rooms $760. A four-room frame house with fireplace and neat trimmings may be put up for $1,000. Very little shelter is needed for stock; cheap outbuildings will do until perma-nent ones can be afforded. A barbed wire fence with posts say twelve feet apart and strung with four wires around 100 acres will average $100 in cost. Where timber for posts is available close at hand the expense will be much less. The cost of sinking a drive well is quite reasonable.

Fine Markets What are people busy with here? Galveston and Hous-ton have a population of 130,000 people. Galves-ton is the chief seaport of the Texas Coast, and Houston is its main railroad center. There is considerable manufacturing and the carrying trade employs large numbers of people. These persons and the truck farmers, fruit-growers and stock-raisers of the rural districts have a constant, near-by market, with thickly settled central and northern Texas not far away.

The counties of Brazoria, Harris and Galveston are building a system of fine graded roads, part of them shelled, leading to neighboring trade centers. This employs some surplus labor and gives quick and easy access to local markets, while the splendid harbor facilities at Galveston afford the grower of grains and the producer of fruits a seaboard market for his surplus, at seaboard prices, untaxed by rail-way tolls.

17

Good Society Good schools and churches are located in most of the settlements, some of them levying special tax for the support of their educational institutions. New-comers need not fear they will lose sight of the little red school house in the lane. The inhabitants are industrious and law-abiding, and the country is exempt from social disorders of all kinds. It is a good place to come with your family and settle.

The Laws The following property is exempt from forced sale for debt: Homestead of 200 acres and improvements in country, or in city to value of $5,000; all farming tools, library, five milch cows and their calves, two yoke of oxen, two horses, one wagon, one carriage or buggy, twenty hogs and twenty sheep, provisions and forage, also current wages. Homestead can be sold under execution only for purchase money or for material and labor furnished, and then only when contract is separately signed by wife.

Is There Room? You need not fear that fruit culture or general farming is in danger of being overdone for many years. At Algoa, Alvin, Arcadia, Alta Loma, Hitchcock, Manvel, Pearland, Dickinson, North Galveston, La Porte, Clear Creek, Webster and Fairwood there are about 25,000 acres under cultivation. It would hardly make a good-sized cattle ranch up in north Texas.

An Explanation The "Coast Country of Texas" enjoys a large rainfall. The Government record for the last twenty years gives from forty-five to sixty-two inches, well distributed.

The year 1899 was an eventful one; winter and early spring were unusually dry, but sub-irrigation came to the rescue and good crops as usual prevailed.

In June, 1899, the largest rainfall yet recorded was had, resulting in serious damage to crops and stock on the Brazos bottom, where for a hundred miles the negroes who largely cultivate the rich Brazos bottoms for a share of the cotton lost their all and were assisted by the generous citizens of the state and nation. Most of the Texas railroads were also damaged by the washing out of bridges and for ten days traffic was impeded.

These facts were heralded by the press all over the United States, and a false impression was given that the country at large was injured. On the contrary the prairie lands of the "Coast Country" (which include nine-tenths of that rich section) were benefited and the Coast Country cheap prairie lands are now being purchased more rapidly than ever.

Another fact should not be lost sight of. Those rich Brazos bottoms—more rich than the Valley of the Nile—raising a bale and a half of cotton to the acre, have only been thus overflowed four times in the last sixty-six years, in 1833, 1852, 1885, and now in 1899. Only once in every sixteen years, the other fifteen years raising the largest crops known anywhere. There is hardly *any* section in America that from some cause does not lose a crop once in from five to ten years.

This year of 1899 has demonstrated two things: That the prairie lands *never* fail of a crop whether too wet or too dry; also the wonderful recuperative qualities that the soil and semi-tropical climate give to that favored region. Hardly had the waters receded from the bottoms before cotton, corn, kaffir corn and seeds of vegetables of all kinds were promptly furnished the hapless negroes whose crops were destroyed, and now in August of the same year the farms are again green with new crops that will mature in from thirty to one hundred days, sufficient to more than support the families of these people.

The Future
Elsewhere are given in detail the advantages of the flourishing towns that line the Santa Fe right-of-way from Hitchcock to Houston.

Everybody in Texas "pulls" for Texas. Confidence begets confidence. It is the firm belief of every farmer on the Gulf, Colorado & Santa Fe Railway that he either has or will have an orchard or small fruit farm just as good and just as valuable as the finest one growing, and it does not require a very vivid stretch of the imagination to see, within a decade, an unbroken line of manorial gardens, country gentlemen's residences and closely cultivated farms all the way from Virginia Point to Houston.

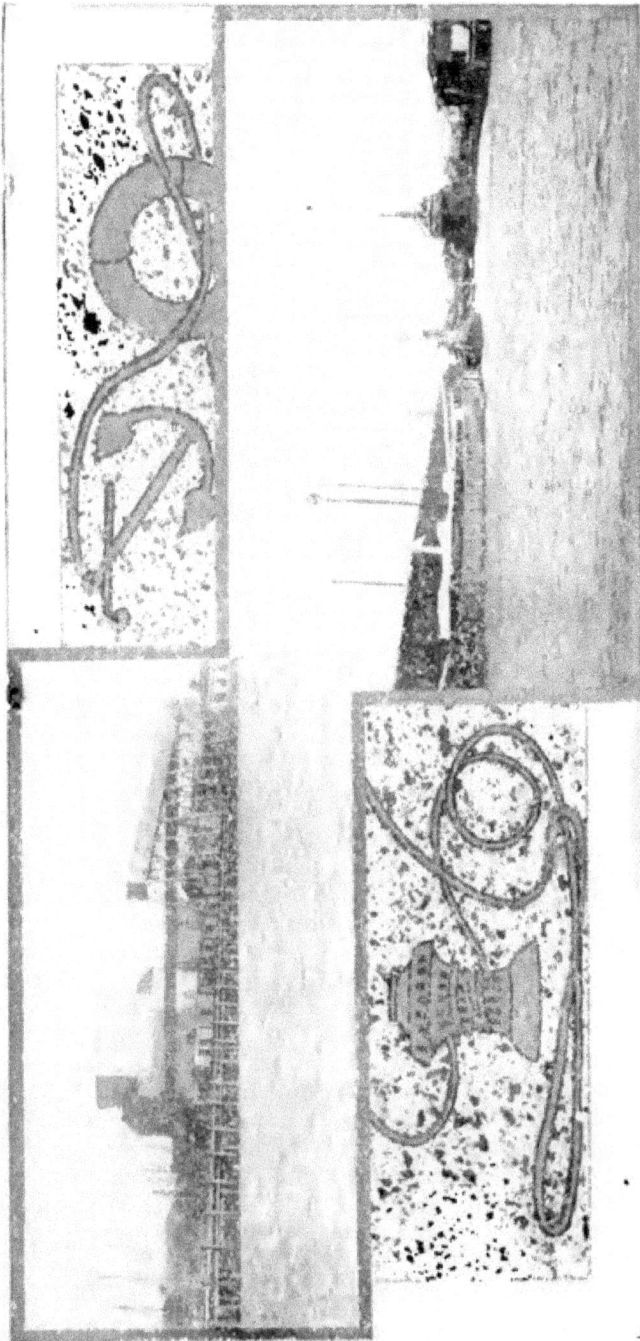

VIEWS ON THE WATERFRONT OF GALVESTON.

Gulf Coast Climate

● ● ●

The temperature along the Gulf Coast of Texas, winter and summer, rarely varies to exceed 15° daily. January is the coldest month in the year; during twenty years the minimum temperature has fallen below 20° in five years only, below 25° in ten years, and below 30° in thirteen years. The temperature along the immediate coast has not reached a maximum of 100° in this period, the highest record being 98° in August, 1874. July is the warmest month. Killing frosts do not usually occur at Houston or Galveston until after December 1 and the unwelcome visitation is frequently delayed until January. Four years in twenty there was no frost whatever at Galveston, and in five different years there was but a single frost. The last hard frost appears any time between January 5 and February 1.

Two Decades Dr. I. M. Cline occupies the position of local forecast official, U. S. Weather Bureau, Galveston. He keeps a careful tab on the daily weather and is authority on the climate of Galveston. As Galveston may fairly be considered representative of the Coast country, his reports from a record of twenty years prior to 1891 are of great interest and value.

Dr. Cline publishes the following statistics with regard to temperature : Normal, 52.3° in January to 84.6° in July; highest monthly mean, 63.7° in February to 86.2° in July; lowest monthly mean, 46.7° in January to 82° in July; maximum (highest) 75° in February to 98° in August; minimum (lowest) 11° in January to 70° in August; greatest monthly range, 26° in February to 58° in January; least monthly range 14° in August to 30° in November. The normal precipitation is 52.48 inches yearly, well distributed through the growing season; average number of clear days per year, 133; average number of partly cloudy days, per year, 140; average number of cloudy days per year, 92; average number of days with some sunshine, 318. Prevailing direction of wind is southeast; average hourly velocity ranges from 8.0 miles in July to 11.9 in January.

Gulf Breezes

The Texas coast winter is more a name than a fact. In summer the weather is without noticeable variation. This evenness of temperature is what makes it possible for the farmer to work comfortably out of doors nearly every day in the year. The genial southern trade wind, blowing over a thousand miles of salt water, brings both warmth and coolness, and contributes to maintain a similarity of seasons. This wind is always in evidence, but rarely moves with enough violence to stir the dust. During a long period, only a few times has it blown a gale, while cyclones are unknown.

No matter how fervent may be the direct rays of the sun, a step into the shade brings pleasant relief. The nights are uniformly agreeable. Occasionally there is a hard frost, preceded by a strong wind from the north. It is the "norther," the fag end of which drops down from snow-covered Dakota prairies to inform Texans that Christmas is coming. Sensitive ears and tender plants have hardly felt its nip when the flurry is over, and the all-pervading Gulf breeze resumes its sway.

Expert's Views

Hon. N. W. McLain, ex-director of the Minnesota state agricultural experiment station, is an enthusiastic convert to the allurements of the Gulf coast climate. In a newspaper article he says:

"Many of those who have lived there for years, speak confidently concerning the general healthfulness of this region, daily visited by the salt sea air. The trade-winds blow every day from the Gulf. They dispense life to vegetation and health to the inhabitants, wherever they reach. The long summers characteristic of this latitude, are by them rendered not only endurable but enjoyable.

"On Christmas Eve it seemed strange to see barefooted boys gazing at Santa Claus and his reindeer flying over artificial snow in the shop windows in Houston; and the salutation, 'Merry Christmas' sounded like a joke at a funeral. On New Years day, it seemed rather unseasonable to sit without a coat or hat, on a porch literally covered with roses, and elegant Marechal Niels blooming out on the lawn. On the twelfth of January I pulled oranges from fine old trees, among the most luxuriant gardens and lawns in Victoria. The nineteenth day of

January I walked through a small field of alfalfa sown the twenty-eight day of last October. The growth completely covered the ground, and the plants averaged eighteen inches in height. January 22d, in the gardens and fields near Alvin, I found the people picking strawberries."

No Malaria Malaria is not prevalent in the country except when invited by carelessness or ignorance. Though this is a flat region, it has but few tracts of swampy land of small extent. Where forests occur, along the bayous, they are devoid of undergrowth; a sign that nothing is present productive of ague. The surplus rainfall drains into the Gulf—chills and fever only appearing sporadically along overflowed and undrained river bottoms. On the high open prairies, malaria is an almost unknown visitor, except where water is permitted to remain stagnant.

Colds and catarrh cause more suffering and deaths in the New England states alone, than the combined diseases of the Gulf Coast. No deadly epidemic diseases have visited this section for a quarter of a century. Periodical fevers are almost entirely absent.

Houston Galveston and Houston are both healthful cities. Dr. Robt. McElroy, city health officer at Houston, says :

" The health of the city of Houston compares favorably with any city in the United States, the death rate for 1898 being very small, undoubtedly caused by better sewage, more paved streets and the universal use of artesian water. Our death rate for the four past years was as follows: 1895, 13.5 per 1,000; 1896, 10.4; 1897, 13.5; 1898, 9.7. Malaria is comparatively unknown now, due principally to use of artesian water, of which there is an inexhaustible supply. Better surface drainage and sewerage also adds much to our improved condition. Contagious diseases are comparatively unknown. Our mild climate, cool Gulf breezes and freedom from sudden changes in temperature makes Houston one of the most desirable places to live in found anywhere in the South."

Galveston From a recent report issued by Dr. W. C. Fisher, health officer, Galveston, it is learned that the general health of that city has been good, notwithstanding the outbreak of dengue fever during the fall of 1897. Statistics show that out of a population of 50,000 there were only 166 deaths during the months of August, September and October, 1897, as against 175 in 1896 and 187 in 1895. This too with a growing population.

Increased sanitary efficiency has brought about this condition of affairs. When the $300,000 appropriated for municipal sewerage has been spent, the general healthfulness of Galveston will be even better.

During 1897 the death rate per thousand was a fraction under 14, and considerably less for 1898, which is a good showing.

It is noteworthy that typhoid fever, diphtheria, scarlet fever, cholera infantum, and other like diseases are almost unknown here. For example, there were only twenty deaths from typhoid, scarlet and malarial fever, and but eight from diphtheria in that year.

Finally The summers in Texas come early and stay late. If that long succession of warm and sunshiny days when one instinctively seeks the shady side of the street becomes monotonous to those who cannot get away for a summer vacation, there is, to offset this, only two months of winter, and that resembles a northern October.

You will like it here when once acquainted. There is a fascination in what at first sight appears undesirable. The soothing Gulf airs are a perpetual invitation to cease worry and fret and hurry. They call to just enough indolence to prevent the human machine from too hastily wearing out.

It is not a misdemeanor to be a trifle lazy in Texas.

Towns and Colonies
● ● ●

Below may be found a detailed description of the more important cities, towns and colonies situated on or contiguous to the Gulf, Colorado & Santa Fe Railway in the Gulf Coast country. The various Mennonite colonies are mentioned elsewhere.

Algoa The town of Algoa and its fruit land suburbs lies on the main line of the Gulf, Colorado & Santa Fe Railway, midway between Houston and Galveston. The location is a favorable one, both as regards quality of soil and nearness to important markets. The town proper is growing nicely, but no effort has been made to boom it—rather it has been the desire to first settle up the fertile surrounding country. A first-class shelled road leads from Algoa over a free wagon bridge to Galveston, so that products can be rapidly handled either by rail or wagon.

Some 2,000 acres of land adjoining Algoa have been platted into small tracts, ranging in size from two to forty acres. Each tract fronts on a public road and all are within one and a quarter miles of the station. The object has been to make this an ideal place for orchards, gardens, etc. There will be no taxes to pay here until the year 1900. Prices of land are governed by location; liberal terms offered actual settlers.

Alta Loma Alta Loma (population 700) is the first station beyond Hitchcock, being seventeen miles from Galveston, on the main Gulf, Colorado & Santa Fe line. It is the center of the Gulf Coast's magnificent fruit belt—a high prairie, heavily sodded with native grasses, and draining to the Gulf by an almost imperceptible descent.

The soil is a black sandy loam, several feet thick, with a yellowish clay subsoil, all underlaid with coarse gravel.

Alta Loma has plenty of pure fresh water, obtained from artesian wells at a depth of 550 to 700 feet. In this vicinity are nineteen artesian wells. The water works for the city of Galveston were

25

RESIDENCES AT ALTA LOMA AND ALVIN.

located here at a cost of about a million dollars. Five million gallons of water are delivered in the city every twenty-four hours.

The entire tract of 8,000 acres is surveyed into subdivisions of ten, twenty and forty acres, and is traversed by roads so arranged as to afford every ten-acre parcel easy access to the station.

Alta Loma has a fine public school building with an attendance of 200 children; has two churches, Baptist and Presbyterian; has a first-class canning factory and preserving works, the plant representing an outlay of more than $10,000 and doing a prosperous business; also has a shirt and overall factory employing quite a number of operatives. The township has about thirty miles of graded roads and a fine system of drainage. Hundreds of acres are now planted in fruit trees, vegetables and flower gardens. "Alta Loma," in the language of its founder, "has not a man, woman or child but what is well clothed and well fed. Its people are healthy, prosperous, law-abiding and happy."

Alvin In Brazoria County, near Mustang Bayou, surrounded by fertile prairies, and at the junction of the Gulf, Colorado & Santa Fe main line and Houston branch, is the wide-awake city of Alvin. Its present population is estimated at 2,000 people, chiefly acquired within the past seven years. There are about 5,000 people within three miles of the center of town. All kinds of retail business are fully represented. Alvin now has several spacious school buildings, several at-

A DOORYARD AT ALVIN.

tractive church edifices, and no saloons.

The Methodist College for Southern Texas and Louisiana is located here. Ice factory plants, two cotton gins and a vinegar establishment are recent acquisitions, brick and drain tile works and a canning factory are assured. Several substantial brick business houses are being erected, and franchises have been granted for electric lighting, street car lines and a telephone exchange. There is an abundance of pure, palatable water, obtainable at a depth of 15 to 20 feet, and several strong flowing wells of choice artesian water.

The climate of this nook is even and healthy, being pleasantly affected, summer and winter, by the Gulf breezes. The soil is a dark, sandy loam, with clay sub-soil, underlaid at a depth of 10 or 15 feet with water-bearing quicksand. Average annual rainfall is 45 inches.

The LeConte and Keifer pears here find a congenial home. Peaches, apricots and plums are successfully grown, and the Japan orange is being introduced. Grapes are a success, the dreaded grape rot being practically unknown. Strawberries do well, if the ground is properly prepared, the fruit ripening in January and continuing to yield until June. It is not uncommon to pick ripe strawberries here Christmas day. The cape jessamine is extensively cultivated around Alvin, forming an important product. All kinds of vegetables flourish—in fact, the briny atmosphere, sandy soil and early seasons make this the truck farmers' gold mine, two or three crops a year being easily grown. Three crops of Irish potatoes are frequently raised in one season. Dairy products command good prices, and poultry-raising is a source of profit.

The nearness of Houston and Galveston, with ample service over the Santa Fe Route, supplemented by excellent country roads, brings Alvin in close touch with unexcelled local markets. The privilege of attaching loaded cars to the fast freight train for northern points is assisting fruit and vegetable growers. In 1898 the shipments by express from Alvin to northern and eastern markets amounted to 15,164 crates of strawberries, covering a fruiting season of more than eighty days. The cash prices ranged from $4.00 to $4.50 up to March 10th, $3.50 for the next two weeks, $3.00 for the following two weeks and $2.75 for final clean up—as compared with only $1.50 per crate in many berry districts.

Amsterdam

Amsterdam is located twelve miles south of Alvin, in the southeastern part of Brazoria County. This town was started three years ago by the Texas Colonization Co., which owns a large adjoining tract.

This is an exceptional body of land, owing to proximity to the Gulf and excellent drainage as well as the superior quality of the soil. Prices range from $12.50 to $15 per acre, on very favorable terms to actual settlers. To get to this property buy a ticket over the Santa Fe Route and get off at Alvin, taking a private conveyance thence to Amsterdam.

Arcadia Arcadia was settled in the spring of 1890. It is situated on the line of the Gulf, Colorado & Santa Fe Railway, twenty-one miles from Galveston, and twenty-nine feet above sea level. The soil is a sandy and black loam, underlaid with yellow clay. For vegetables the sandy loam is generally preferred, though both are good for fruits.

The whole country is sub-irrigated at a depth of five or six feet, rendering it drouth proof so far as trees are concerned, although even vegetables rarely suffer.

Artesian water can be had at a depth of 100 to 600 feet, the quality being better at the greater depths. Every variety of vegetable succeeds well. Tomatoes ripen by the middle of May; strawberries are ready for picking last of February, and bear abundantly until June, a yield of $150 to $300 per acre not being uncommon. LeConte and Keifer pears are always vigorous, absolutely healthy, and bear an average of eight bushels to each tree six years old. American grapes are uniformly healthy, productive and free from rot or mildew. Cotton does well without manuring, the yield ranging from one-half to a full bale, and in lower locations sugar-cane is a success; it is not hurt by frost before the first of December and rarely prior to the middle of January. Pears have been planted here on 3,000 acres and peaches on 200 acres. The largest orchards are owned by B. F. Johnson, C. Peterson, J. Wharton Terry, C. E. Angell and E. C. Lamb.

There is no malaria, the sea breeze sweeping it away. Land is for sale at reasonable prices.

Arcola Arcola, in Fort Bend County, is the name of a pretty town on the Gulf, Colorado & Santa Fe Railway, where that road connects with the International & Great Northern and the Sugarland & Arcola Railways. This promising place is eighteen miles from Houston and forty-three miles from Galveston.

DECEMBER VIEW OF A HOME IN ARCADIA

The country round about is filling up with a desirable class of farmers, more than one hundred families having settled here. Here is the dividing line between the immense stretch of black prairie extending eastward to Galveston Bay and the bottom lands of Oyster Creek and Brazos River on the west. West of Arcola the bottom lands have been utilized as cotton, sugar and corn plantations; they are now being divided into farm tracts and rapidly taken up by small farmers. The eastern prairies were originally devoted to the grazing of cattle; these also are being placed upon the market in small holdings.

Good drinking and stock water is obtained anywhere in the Arcola region at a depth of 20 to 40 feet. Pure artesian water flows freely when tapped 300 to 800 feet below the surface.

Nearly everything grows here. Cotton makes one bale to the acre; the corn product is 40 to 50 bushels per acre; oats are a success, the annual yield per acre averaging 60 to 75 bushels.

At Arcola is located the sugar plantation and factory of J. H. B. House. Cane yields 20 to 30 tons per acre and the factories pay about $3 per ton for it.

Truck gardening is also quite remunerative. Beans, onions, peas, cabbage, potatoes, beets, tomatoes, melons, etc., grow to perfection and bring high prices in adjacent markets. From $200 to $500 can be made from a winter garden of two acres, and the same ground planted in summer with grains. Pears, strawberries and all kinds of fruit do well. Tame grasses—timothy, crimson clover, bermuda and alfalfa—are successfully grown.

Arcola has three railroads, two sugar factories, a lumber yard, two hotels and livery stable. It desires a general store, cotton gin, newspapers, brickyard, drug store, canning factory and floral garden.

Edna Edna, Jackson County (population 2,000) lies near the waters of Matagorda Bay, but has little water front, thus being beyond the range of any coast storms. The land is level. Much of it needs artificial drainage to become productive; this can easily be accomplished by taking advantage of the many fresh water creeks, such as Mustang, Sandy, Navidad, Lavaca, Arenosa, Benan,

Coxe's and Keller. These streams are skirted with timber, furnishing an abundance of fuel and fence posts. About 70 per cent. is prairie and 30 per cent. timber.

The soil is fertile, producing corn, cotton, vegetables and fruits; corn yields an average per acre of 30 bushels; sweet potatoes, 200 bushels; prairie hay, one ton, and cotton 300 pounds. With proper cultivation pears are particularly successful. Good water is plentiful. The climate is healthful.

Edna, the county seat, is located on the line of the Southern Pacific Co. sixty-seven miles west of Rosenberg. It is a growing town of 1,500 inhabitants, closely in touch with the surrounding country. Edna's public schools, churches and stores are far above the average.

Unimproved lands, in tracts of almost any size, may be bought at $4 to $10 per acre. Higher prices are charged for lands near the county seat and railroad, or for improved farms. Prospective settlers in the Coast Region of Texas are invited to examine what is offered in the vicinity of Edna, in case they should not find exactly what is wanted at a point nearer the Gulf, Colorado & Santa Fe Railway

El Campo

Seven years ago there was no El Campo. Today the town has a population of over 1,200. More than twenty new business enterprises have been established here within the past year. Wharton County is being rapidly populated by a very enterprising class of people, largely consisting of Swedes. There are very few negroes.

Around El Campo is some of the richest soil in Texas, high and comparatively dry. The surrounding country, which was once a large cattle pasture, is being divided into fruit and cotton farms.

El Campo has butchers, bakers, lumbermen, bankers, grocers—in fact every leading branch of trade is represented. The New York, Texas & Mexican Railway furnishes good shipping facilities.

The business district is composed of substantial wooden structures of modern architecture, while large, spacious churches have been erected by several denominations.

Fairbanks Fairbanks is located twelve miles northwest of Houston, on the Houston & Texas Central Railroad and on the main county thoroughfare, called the Washington County Road. This is now macadamized out from Houston to within three miles of Fairbanks. Work is rapidly progressing on about five miles more.

The land in that vicinity is a black, sandy loam, mostly prairie, with strips of timber along the creeks. The elevation is from five to eight feet to the mile, which affords excellent natural drainage in connection with the railroad and county road ditches running through the center of the property, and a creek on either side.

The lands around the town are being rapidly settled by thrifty northern farmers, who seem to be contented and doing well. The prices range from $5 to $10 per acre. There is a sawmill and planing mill within four miles of Fairbanks, which supplies cheap building material. The best of well water can be had at the depth of 15 to 30 feet at a cost of 50 cents per foot with pipe and pump all complete.

A general store and lumber yard, carpenter and blacksmith shops, school, postoffice, depot and express office are part of the conveniences of the town. Newcomers have organized and expect to raise vegetables and melons in quantities, so that they can ship in carload lots to northern markets. Some of the finest vegetables and melons on the Houston market in the past three years were raised at Fairbanks, and a number of carloads were shipped to northern markets with very satisfactory results.

33

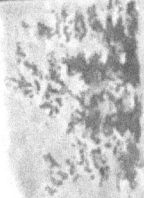

Mr. C. W. Hahl has several acres of canaigre planted which is doing nicely, and promises to be a profitable crop; this is used for tanning purposes. It is becoming very popular where introduced and the demand cannot be supplied. The profit per acre, at a conservative estimate is from $.40 to $50.

Galveston

Great cities rise and flourish in response to a need. Rarely are they created by individual fiat or caprice.

Galveston supplies a distinct want, that of ocean port for the Southwest, and therefore will grow steadily year by year, keeping pace with the territory it serves. The city is built on the extreme eastern end of Galveston Island, just off the Gulf Coast of Texas, is six miles in area, and has a population of nearly 65,000.

This fact appears remarkable; that a city of that size should transact business equal to other communities with three or four times more inhabitants. The anomaly is easily explained. The finest land-locked harbor on the Gulf of Mexico has given Galveston an immense carrying trade. Here come ships from European and South American ports to carry away cotton, corn and wheat, in exchange for money or foreign commodities. So profitable has been the handling of these exchanges that conservative merchants and brokers were content to reap assured gains without seeking to bring in strangers by heralding to the outside world the city's manifest advantages. Already this is the third richest city in the United States according to population.

Galveston was not discovered in the true sense of the word, until a few years ago. Then the great West awoke to the fact that by means of the Santa Fe Route it was linked to a first-class deep water port, the largest and deepest on the Gulf Coast, several hundred miles nearer the interior than is New York City. For example: Galveston is 220 miles nearer to St. Louis, 739 miles nearer Denver and 483 miles nearer Kansas City than New York is.

The United States Government estimates that $6,200,000 is required to secure a channel of sufficient depth across the bar at the entrance of the bay. Now there is more than 27 feet of water at average tides, which will be increased to accommodate any craft that floats. Jetty construction was begun in 1885, but work was not actually pushed until 1890.

The south jetty is seven and one-half miles long and the north arm has been extended nearly six miles.

During 1896 there arrived at Galveston 28 vessels from foreign ports, of which number one-sixth carried cargoes, not including the small local craft. The clearances were 303, all with cargoes. The number of vessels entered in the coastwise business that year was 369. A gratifying increase in ocean trade is reported for 1898. As an exporting city Galveston ranks fourth or fifth, and has regular steamer lines to Houston, Key West, New York, Brazos, Santiago and Morgan City; also between Galveston and the foreign ports of Hamburg, Bremen, Antwerp, Liverpool, Manchester, Tampico and Vera Cruz.

Four miles of completed wharves, on the bay

COTTON WHARF, GALVESTON.

front, with room for more, amply accommodate existing traffic. Four immense grain elevators have been erected, with storage capacity of 2,500,000 bushels; other elevators are projected. During the commercial season, after September 1, the docks are filled with bales of cotton. Cotton is the chief staple of Texas and half of it comes to Galveston, making this the first cotton port of America, an honor previously belonging to New Orleans, the value of Galveston cotton exports, season of 1898-1899, being $51,271,392, against New Orleans' $35,355,-647, the former gaining nearly $12,000,000 and the latter losing $10,000,000 in comparison with 1897-1898—a remarkable showing. Every bale of cotton

ONE OF THE GALVESTON ELEVATORS.

leaves in the city from $1 to $1.50 to pay for handling, wharfage, etc.

Cotton and woolen mills, bagging, binding, twine,
rope and lace factories are established here; the total
of manufacturing establishments is 43. The fish
and oyster business will soon rival that of Baltimore.

The total exports for 1896 amounted to $56,000,-
000, customs-house receipts for 1896, $191,945.
These figures give a fair idea of the business passing through Galveston.

Hon. A. J. Rosenthal, deputy collector of cus-
toms, has compiled the following interesting additional data respecting Galveston's commerce:

"The tonnage of vessels which have entered this
port for the last three years was as follows: 1898,
899,112 tons; 1897, 642,465 tons; 1896, 496,045
tons. It is to be taken into consideration that
during the months of our war with Spain the coastwise trade with New York and Boston was entirely
suspended.

The following table shows some of the exports
from the farms of the State of Texas, via Galveston:

COTTON.—1898, 1,982,618 bales, 1,557,480,207
lbs., $55,789,071 value; 1897, 1,380,728 bales,
724,882,228 lbs., $53,641,284 value; 1896, 1,159,895
bales, 614,744,456 lbs., $49,179,556 value.

COTTONSEED MEAL AND CAKE.—1898, 519,375,-
071 lbs., $4,350,526 value; 1897, 373,665,521 lbs.,
$2,939,312 value; 1896, 306,691,523 lbs., $3,060,900
value.

37

COTTONSEED OIL.—1898, 9,761,567 gals., $2,-483,824 value; 1897, 4,431,001 gals., $1,181,000 value; 1896, 1,936,499 gals., $484,125 value.

COTTONSEED.—1898, 2,872,580 lbs., $17,317 value.

BREADSTUFFS.—1898, $12,195,322 value; 1897, $8,269,951 value; 1896, $4,291,668 value.

VALUE OF LIVE STOCK.—1898, $77,141,816; 1897, $60,965,060; 1896, $55,999,228.

VALUE OF FOREIGN IMPORTS.—1898, $2,586,300; 1897, $644,237; 1896, $794,908; 1895, $337,178.

GRAND TOTALS.

	VESSELS.	TONS.	EXPORTS.	IMPORTS.
1898	759	1,214,013	877,148,836	$2,586,300
1897	705	1,036,522	60,965,060	644,237
1896	613	844,426	55,999,228	794,908

COMPARISON OF CASH RECEIPTS JANUARY AND FEBRUARY, 1898-1899.

1899, Jan., $23,327.18;   1898, Jan., $19,699.31
1899, Feb., 18,990.51;   1898, Feb.,   9,475.00

Net increase in Custom House receipts $13,143.38 in two months.

Another factor of Galveston's prosperity is its selection as headquarters for general offices and shops of the Santa Fe System in Texas. Handsome and substantial business blocks compactly line several wide streets, and merchants appear to be prospering. The many beautiful homes, fine churches, and numerous schools of Galveston attest its superior advantages as a residence city. Several large hotels invite and foster transient custom. Many residents of the interior Texas towns spend their summers in this delightful spot, invigorated by the cool sea breeze; and in the winter

TWO-YEAR OLD PEACH TREE AT WEBSTER.

A GALVESTON WHARF SCENE.

invalids and pleasure seekers drop down from the North to enjoy May weather in December.

To miss seeing Galveston is not to have seen a representative Texas City.

Hitchcock Hitchcock, in Galveston County, on main line of Gulf, Colorado & Santa Fe Railway, fourteen miles from Galveston, is the original home of the pear industry in Texas. Here formerly lived the eminent horticulturist H. M. Stringfellow, who first discovered that this section could produce with profit the finest pears in the world. His attractive home, beautiful grounds and well-kept orchards attest the admirable qualities of this place. The original Stringfellow orchard now includes probably the largest nursery in Texas; its beauty attracts many visitors.

Numerous strawberry patches and truck farms lie within a radius of three miles. The land is sub-irrigated. Good well water is found at a depth of twelve to eighteen feet, and there are thirteen artesian wells, varying in depth from 400 to 700 feet, with a flow ranging from 45 to 145 gallons per minute—the water rising twenty-five and thirty-five feet above ground.

Several large rose nurseries are located here. Judge Austin owns a fine nursery, containing 30,000 roses and 1,000 magnolias. W. L. Schumate and Capt. J. Aiken have 250,000 rose bushes, and F. Renaud 30,000. Tourists can obtain, in season, beautiful bouquets of rosebuds to take north, if orders are placed a day ahead. Cape jessamines are a decided success at Hitchcock, and the Satsuma variety of Japan orange is quite popular.

Over 1,000 acres of the country immediately tributary to Hitchcock are planted with pear trees, 100 acres with strawberries, 100 acres with grapes and 500 acres are devoted to cultivation of other fruits and vegetables. H. N. Lowrey, three miles west of Hitchcock, has planted 10,000 pear trees, 3,000 peach trees and 4,000 plum trees. The Wheeler Fruit Company has 11,000 pear trees and 25 acres in strawberries.

Persons desiring to invest in small fruit farms will do well to visit Hitchcock. At this point and Alvin enough has been accomplished to prove beyond cavil, that the coast country of Texas cannot be surpassed for productiveness.

Houston If steamships made Galveston, railroads have made Houston—that prosperous and beautiful city of over 72,000 people which has grown up at the head of tide-water navigation, fifty-five miles from the head of the jetties at Bolivar Peninsula. The LVth Congress appropriated $377,000 for immediate use out of the $4,000,000 required to make a channel from the Galveston jetties to the harbor near the heart of this city. This government work, when completed, will allow the largest ocean going vessels to meet Houston's fourteen railroads. As a result the anomaly will be presented of an important transportation and commercial inland city with 14 miles of harbor. That vessels can be sheltered by a " land-locked harbor " in fresh water is a fact of importance to navigators.

BUFFALO BAYOU, HOUSTON.

The city was founded in 1821 and has grown from 29,000 inhabitants in 1890 to its present size. Nearby are immense forests of pine, oak, etc., and the profusion of magnolia groves in the suburbs has given it the name of the " Magnolia City."

These are some of the things that Houston offers the newcomer:

A healthful and enjoyable semi-tropical climate; mean summer temperature of 90° and average winter temperature of 60°; sweet, pure and soft artesian water, a low death rate—less than nine to the

41

LIGHT GUARDS ARMORY.   GOVERNMENT BUILDING AND POST OFFICE.   RESIDENCE OF S. K. DICK.

CITY OF HOUSTON.

thousand—sixty-two miles of paved streets—vitrified brick, stone, wood and asphalt; no stagnant water and an admirable sewerage system; handsome public and business buildings, and many beautiful private residences; large modern hotels, a big convention hall and many beautiful churches; the finest electric street railway system in the south, 46 miles completed; a taxable valuation of $27,000,000, the rate being $2 per $100; a high school and 15 public schools for benefit of 12,000 children.

The bank clearances for 1898 were $306,946,448, an increase of $34,595,466 over 1897, and more than many cities of twice Houston's population. Three million dollars are invested in building associations, $350,000 in transportation lines, and $4,600,000 in manufacturing and industrial establishments, including six cotton compresses and four cotton seed oil mills. There is plenty of money here to do business with.

BUSINESS BLOCK AT HOUSTON.

Fourteen trunk lines of railroad enter Houston, affording ample means for traffic with half of the vast area between the lower Mississippi River and the Pacific. The roads actually centering in this city have a mileage of 5,817 and the connecting systems a mileage of 31,000. Seven of them have their general offices and shops here, disbursing $400,000

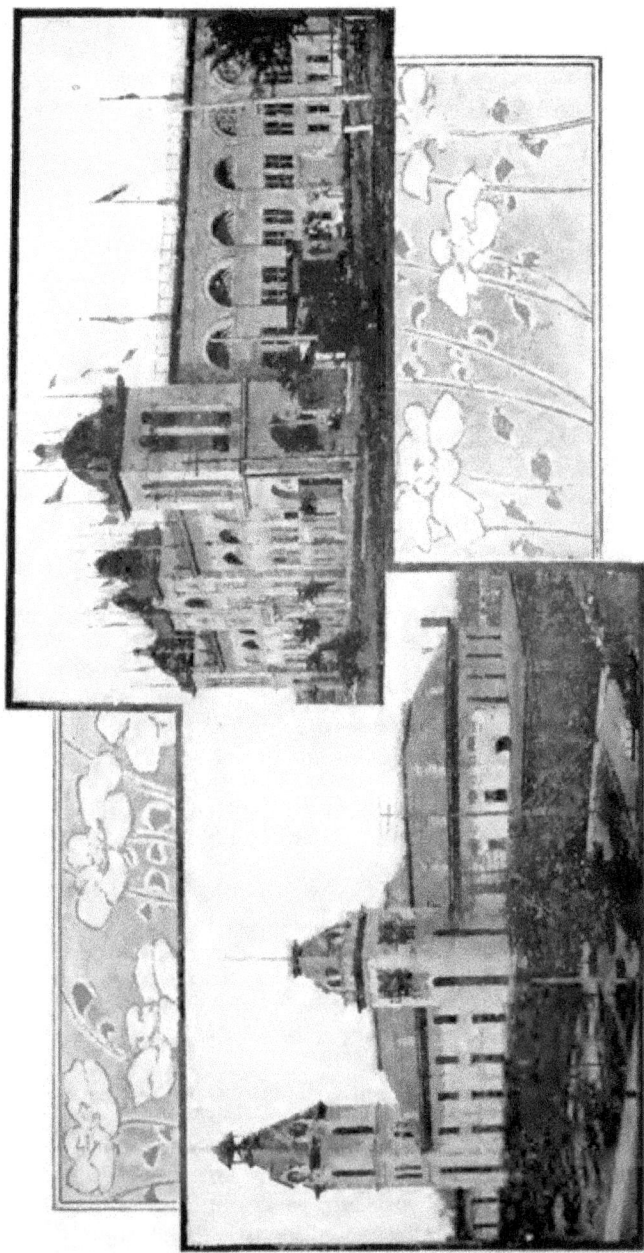

HOUSTON MARKET HOUSE AND AUDITORIUM.

among their employes and officers, and the Santa Fe has erected a commodious passenger depot on Congress street to accommodate its rapidly increasing traffic. Its trains also run into Grand Central Depot. The Santa Fe is the popular line between Houston and Galveston.

The jobbing houses of Houston do an immense business ($32,000,000 annually) among the timber regions of East Texas, the central cotton section of the State, and the sugar districts of Texas and southwestern Louisiana. Eighty miles of switches, side-tracks, etc., afford complete facilities for handling freight. In addition to the facilities offered by the Santa Fe Route for rail transportation to seaboard, a system of barges deliver cargoes on board ocean steamers at Galveston without trans-shipment.

Other items of interest are the gas works, with a plant capacity for 100,000 population; public school buildings valued at $365,000, and fine artesian water, the average supply being 3,000,000 gallons, drawn from 39 wells.

As a cotton market Houston takes a front rank. The gross receipts from Sept. 1st, 1898 to March 9th, 1899, were 2,317,715 bales, being an excess of receipts this year over last of 632,804 bales. The increased amount paid for cotton at Houston in 1898 over 1897 was $34,535,466, notwithstanding the low price of that staple. One-third of the cotton crop of America and one-fifth of the cotton crop of the world is raised within 450 miles of Houston and Galveston.

There are 40,000,000 acres of pine timber lands in East Texas and Louisiana, with Houston as headquarters for this immense traffic. The annual lumber trade amounts to over $25,000,000. Twenty-six million dollars worth of traffic was done last year over Buffalo Bayou, Houston's "arm of the sea."

A large trade of the city of Houston is in Texas products, such as cotton, sugar, molasses, melons, rice, fruits, lumber, wool and hides, also fish and oysters. Houston has an enviable future before it, if the growth of the last decade should be continued Its location is such as to command a large share of the industrial prosperity of Southern Texas, and it will always be an important factor in that region.

Acknowledgment is hereby made of the courtesy of Dr. V. S. MacNider and Messrs. Blackburn & Bailey, in furnishing photos of Houston for reproduction herein.

PRESBYTERIAN CHURCH, HOUSTON.

La Porte The confluence of Buffalo Bayou and San Jacinto River form what is known as San Jacinto Bay, a body of fresh water seven miles long by from one to two miles in width. At the lower end it is almost separated from Galveston Bay, the great inland sea of Texas, by a promontory which ranges in width from 1,500 feet at its point to one and one-half miles at its base. This promontory has an elevation of forty feet above San Jacinto Bay, and thirty-five feet above Galveston Bay, the former bank being abrupt, while the latter recedes in graceful, easy terraces almost to the water's edge. Beautiful hardwood trees, green ten months in the year, draped with Spanish moss and mistletoe, fringe the borders of the promontory, and picturesque little islands of the same timber give a most pleasing effect to the general landscape.

By water this promontory is located forty miles

46

from Houston and thirty miles from Galveston, but by rail or wagon road it is but twenty-four miles from Houston and thirty-two miles from Galveston, being practically, either by land or water, midway between the two great cities of Texas.

On this strip of land the town of La Porte is situated. It is already quite a place with ample railroad, navigation, telegraph and telephone facilities. La Porte possesses churches, school-houses, hotels, livery stables, stores of all varieties and well-equipped bathing houses. The surrounding agricultural country (and there is none better in the state) is well developed. The proposed great ship channel will make it an important commercial point.

La Porte is becoming widely known throughout Texas as a delightful summer resort. It is a veritable Coney Island for Houston, and summer excursions from that city are frequent. The hunting and fishing in the fall and winter attract many sportsmen from the North, who often remain for months. The bathing, boating, fishing and sailing facilities are unexcelled.

Surrounding La Porte, together with the adjoining tract of land known as South La Porte, is about 4,000 acres of land, which has been laid off in small tracts for fruit and vegetable farmers. The prices of town lots in La Porte and its neighboring farms are reasonable and the terms easy.

In addition to its properties at La Porte, the American Land Company (with headquarters at Chicago, St. Louis and Houston) also has charge of the tracts at Meadowbrook and Webster; correspondence invited.

Manvel The settlement of Manvel is situated in Brazoria County, on the Gulf, Colorado & Santa Fe Railway main line, midway between Arcola and Alvin, and is thirty-six miles distant from Houston. Two hundred heads of families have settled within a few miles of the depot. Many of them are Dunkards, a religious sect whose industry and thrift are proverbial.

It has been demonstrated that it is as fertile as any other portion of the coast. Nearly 4,000 acres of land has been cut up into ten, twenty and forty acre tracts, lying near the town site, the selling price being $15 to $30 per acre. The summer of 1897 the cultivated acreage was as follows: Pears

DOWN THE PATHS OF PEACE.

and other fruits, 250 acres; strawberries, 100 acres; vegetables, 50 acres.

Cotton is being extensively planted and the region around Manvel bids fair to be as great a cotton and corn country as Northern Texas. The soil is of two kinds, black-sandy and black-waxy, the latter being well adapted for corn and cotton.

Five miles from Manvel is a choice tract of 20,000 acres, in a solid body, located on the west side of Chocolate Bayou. It has been surveyed, sub-divided and platted into lots of forty acres each, with road-ways for everyone, connecting with the main high-way, and so arranged that they can be conveniently cut into smaller lots of ten or twenty acres each.

Meadowbrook

Meadowbrook, Harris County, Texas, consists of about 20,000 acres of land, located in the celebrated South Texas Coast Country, and controlled by the American Land Co. It is within twenty miles of Houston, the county seat, which is the largest city of Texas.

The land is all a beautiful prairie, except that the banks of Buffalo Bayou and its tributaries are fringed with groves of hardwood timber, principally of the several varieties of oak, the utility of which for fuel, fence posts, etc., is apparent. Three railroads and three county roads pass through Meadowbrook, and it is perfectly drained by Buffalo Bayou, one of the important waterways of Texas, passing through the tract from the west to the east. Two railroad stations, with side-track and other shipping facilities, are already situated on Meadowbrook and arrangements are well under the way for the third.

This large body of land has been divided into farms of 160 acres each, and graded roads are being constructed along the section lines, at right angles to Buffalo Bayou, thus affording each quarter section the double purpose of an outlet to the railroads and county roads as well as drainage to the Bayou. The main road from Houston has been graded and grav-eled to within nine miles of Meadowbrook and will be completed in the near future.

Fruits of nearly every variety, both large and small, all kinds of vegetables, and the great staples of cot-ton, corn, oats, sugar and hay give the most grati-fying results at Meadowbrook. Improved farms surrounding this tract show positive evidence as to what can be produced and it has been placed on the market at prices and terms, that, together with its general conditions, invite comparison with any other lands in that most favored portion of these United States.

Pearland The town of Pearland, fifteen miles south of Houston, on the Gulf, Colorado & Santa Fe Railway, is the center of a splendid country. The town-site has been laid off on a modern plan, with boulevards and broad streets, reserving locations for churches and parks. It is expected to build up here a model community. Pearland is surrounded by thousands of acres of the finest prairie land, nearly every acre of which is suited to fruit, vegetable and general farming. Ten thousand acres of the land immediately surrounding Pearland have been sub-divided into ten, twenty and forty-acre tracts, which are being sold at $15 to $25 per acre, one-third cash, the balance in one and two years. Each tract will front a broad, graded road.

Pearland is now a thriving village of 300 inhabitants. It has schools and churches and is surrounded by a desirable class of citizens who are engaged in fruit-raising and general farming. Considering age, Pearland can show one of the finest pear orchards along the coast.

Richmond Richmond is the county seat of Fort Bend County. It is a prosperous and enterprising town, containing about 1,500 people. Its location on the west bank of the Brazos River, within a short distance of the Falls of the Brazos, will give it, when the 3,000 horse power there is fully developed, a commanding position as a manufacturing center.

Richmond is not only a pleasant place in which to live, but it is a good place to do business in. Already the town possesses water works, an electric light plant, bank, three railroads, a telephone exchange, two cotton gins and a grist mill. One notable feature is an immigrant house, where any person who has bought land in the county or who deposits a certain amount of money in bank is granted free house rent for a month or so in order to make ready for the occupancy of his new home.

Not content with being in the center of a magnificent agricultural country, Richmond is reaching out for various enterprises and affords excellent opportunities for the location of manufactories based on cotton, timber and sugar.

Rosenberg

Rosenberg is very favorably situated in Fort Bend County, at the junction of the main lines of the Gulf, Colorado & Santa Fe Railway and Southern Pacific Co. It is also the northern terminus of the New York, Texas & Mexican Railway, and the Rosenberg, Damon Mound & Gulf Railroad. It lies 66 miles north of Galveston and 36 miles west of Houston; contains 750 inhabitants (mainly from northern states) and is the natural trade center of a rich country. This outlying territory consists of say 400 sections of high prairie lands and rich river bottoms where, without fertilizing, the average crops are forty bushels of corn, seventy bushels of oats, three tons of millet hay and one bale of cotton per acre. All kinds of fruits—except apples—are raised here, as well as all varieties of vegetables.

The Brazos River bottoms contain great forests of oak, ash and other hard woods, interspersed with magnificent plantations where corn, cotton and sugar cane grow luxuriantly. Desirable farming lands lying within a radius of three to eight miles from town command $8 to $25 per acre. Taxes are low, about $1 per hundred on a 40% valuation.

Rosenberg has several church societies and fine school buildings. Being 132 feet above sea level and 40 feet above the Brazos, good drainage and consequent good health is assured. Excellent water is obtainable at convenient depths.

Its location in the midst of forests of red and white cedar, cypress, ash, etc., makes Rosenberg a desirable place for the manufacture of woolen goods. A canning factory would also do well here. The transportation facilities above mentioned give this town manifest advantages as a distributing point. Persons desiring further information should address Geo. B. Lang, Secretary Progressive Association, Rosenberg, Texas.

Sealy

The thriving town of Sealy is situated fifty miles west of Houston and ninety-five miles northwest of Galveston at the junction of the

Gulf, Colorado & Santa Fe Railway and the Missouri, Kansas & Texas Railroad, and has a population of about 1,500. It is the first division on the Santa Fe line out of Galveston, with a round-house and other necessary improvements.

The town is situated on a slight elevation above the surrounding country, just at the beginning of the rolling land adjacent to the coast country proper, thereby having excellent natural drainage and splendid water, and is one of the healthiest places in South Texas. The Brazos River is five miles distant. Sealy possesses a first-class public school system and churches of the various denominations.

The citizens liberally support a weekly newspaper, and the town boasts of a tannery, harness and saddle manufactory, a mattress factory, also two of the finest steam cotton gins in this part of the country, one of them having just lately been purchased to be put in operation this summer. A complete electric plant of 700 light capacity is building. A commodious opera house and public amusement hall, five first-class hotels, besides numerous business edifices, complete the list of principal buildings.

In addition to the magnificent resources of Austin County elsewhere briefly alluded to, it may be said that the excellent railroad facilities at Sealy make the raising of canteloupes and watermelons one of the leading industries of the region. About 500 acres of melons will be marketed at Sealy this year to be shipped north. The value of adjacent farming lands varies from $5 to $40 per acre.

Superior Lies thirty-three miles from Galveston, twenty miles from Houston, and begins just two miles north of Alvin, on the Houston branch of the Santa Fe, with eight daily passenger trains. This is a new town located upon a tract of 10,000 acres of land purchased by the Southern Homestead Company of Houston, and characterized as the finest large body of land along the Gulf Coast. It is in the center of the newly developed fruit and vegetable belt and is being highly improved with finely graded roads and ample ditches. Many settlers have located at this place.

Wallis The thrifty town of Wallis (population 500) is located in Austin County, at the junction of the San Antonio & Aransas Pass Railway

with the Gulf, Colorado & Santa Fe Railway,
eighty-two miles north of Galveston and forty-five
miles west of Houston. Its twenty business houses
carry large stocks of goods and it has a wide-awake
newspaper. Educational and social advantages are
as advanced as those of any like settlement in Southern Texas. Railroad facilities are unusually good.

Austin County is briefly described under another
caption. A few additional facts pertaining especially
to the territory surrounding Wallis will be of interest.
The lands between the Brazos and San Bernard Rivers are of inexhaustible fertility, being as rich now
as when first cultivated forty years ago. The prairie
lands are worth $5 to $20 per acre; bottom lands,
$10 to $30.

Cotton is a crop that never fails. In 1897 Wallis
marketed 5,000 bales. In a good season the output
is about 8,000 bales. Corn averages 40 to 60 bushels to the acre. Vegetables and small fruits are successfully raised. The country around Wallis is in-
habited to a considerable extent by Germans, who
with their customary industry have made valuable
improvements. Homeseekers who prefer to get back
from the Coast and at the same time have the bene-
fit of the Gulf breezes, should investigate the claims
of Wallis and vicinity.

Webster The colony of Webster, Harris
County, Texas, is located on a tract
of about 5,000 acres of land midway between Houston and Galveston, on the line of the Galveston,
Houston & Henderson Railroad, over which also
operates two other lines, thus practically affording
it the advantages of three railroads. It has a depot,
side-track and other ample shipping facilities. Population about 300.

This is a magnificent body of black prairie land,
perfectly drained, and is in the midst of the great
fruit and vegetable district of South Texas. Well
developed farms in and surrounding Webster evidence its great productiveness. Clear Lake, a navigable stream and tributary of Galveston Bay, directly
adjoins this land and its settlers have all the advantages of water competition. Real estate at Webster
will be sold in tracts to suit the purchaser and at
very reasonable prices and terms, considering the
location.

This year more than 400 acres around Webster

are planted in nutmeg melons—the Rocky Ford variety—and the entire crop contracted in advance.

Wharton Rosenberg station, on the Gulf, Colorado & Santa Fe Railway, is the most convenient point of departure for a large section of country to the southwest. After passing through Fort Bend County, the next one is Wharton, dubbed by its enthusiastic inhabitants the banner county of the coast country. It is in the second tier back from the Gulf. The county is watered by Peach, Jones, Sandies and Mustang creeks, also the Bernard and Colorado Rivers. Wharton contains 1,172 square miles, a princely domain of 718,000 acres, three-eighths woodland and five-eighths open country; surface is level, divided equally between prairie and woodland; soil is alluvial and adapted to almost everything that grows in the south. Along the Colorado River especially the soil is of great depth. On the water courses there is a sufficiency of timber for firewood. Railroad facilities are excellent, the county being traversed by three lines. The average annual yield in Wharton County is 20,000 bales of cotton, 200,000 bushels of corn, 20,000 bushels of Irish potatoes, over 10,000 bushels of sweet potatoes, 20 cars of pecans, etc. Being in the fruit belt, everything of that kind does well here. Unimproved lands bring $5 to $15 per acre; improved, $15 to $30.

The town of Wharton, county seat, stands on the east bank of the Colorado River, 50 miles from the coast. It is the principal distributing point for Wharton and Matagorda counties. Present population, 2,000. Its business establishments have a heavy trade, and the social and educational advantages of the town have kept pace with its industrial growth.

BOOTH'S ORCHARD, CLEAR CREEK.

Mennonite Colonies

• • •

The present exodus of Mennonites from various
northern states to Southern Texas is in many respects
a remarkable movement. Nothing like it has been
witnessed for many years.

These Mennonites are a thrifty people, noted as
home-builders. By hard work, prudence and fore-
sight they have made a success of nearly all their
undertakings. It seems to be their mission to be
pioneers of farming industry.

They are an exceptional race. Piety and practical
affairs go hand in hand While fearing God they do
not fear Nature. No unfavorable combination of
soil or climate or circumstances has ever routed them.
They may leave one locality for another, but the
migration is based on other grounds than failure at
home. Each change is a step forward.

They are withal shrewd buyers, investigating carefully before pulling up stakes and starting anew. So
well known is their sagacity in this respect that keen
competition exists among holders of large bodies of
raw lands whenever it is known that a new Mennonite enterprise is to be launched. It is a compliment
to the resources of any country to be selected by the
Mennonites for colonizing purposes, because by experience they have learned what good land is and
will have no other.

Mr. W. B. Slosson, of Houston, Texas, who is at
present the authorized general agent for the Mennonite colonies at Ft. Bend, Thompson or Menno
City, Westfield and Brookshire, was instrumental in
bringing down to the Texas Gulf Coast more than
a thousand Mennonites during the fall of 1897.
More than 400 have already located and many
others are coming in from far away Oregon, South
Dakota, Minnesota, Illinois and Iowa, as well as from
Nebraska, Kansas, Oklahoma and Northern Texas.
Mr. Slosson has acted in conjunction with a Committee of Eleven, many of them Mennonite preachers
and all men of influence. The Santa Fe Route was
unanimously chosen by them as the "official line" for
transportation of settlers and goods, thereby further

cementing a friendship which began when the Santa Fe brought the Mennonites over from Russia to America many years ago.

The question may be asked: Why are these people leaving their northern homes and coming so far south? An important reason is that the good cheap lands of the Middle West are almost gone and the tide of immigration must seek other outlets. One of these outlets is towards Southern Texas. For years the coast region was owned and controlled by cattle men; they did not want their great pastures cut up into small holdings. That day has passed, and they are inviting rather than repelling the advent of the farmer and fruit-raiser.

Another factor is found in the movement for deepwater harbors at Galveston, Houston and other points on the Texas coast, permitting the immense surplus crops of the northwest and southwest to be more easily and profitably marketed than heretofore. This has widely advertised Southern Texas.

Other reasons, as detailed by the committee in their literature, may be briefly summed up in the items of "a healthy climate, good water, excellent markets, no blizzards, sufficient rainfall, low taxes, cheap freight rates, cool Gulf breezes in summer, scarcely any winter, fruit culture successful, a diversity of crops possible, more than one crop a year obtainable in some instances, friendly neighbors, and an opportunity to build up a prosperous community of those holding the same faith and swayed by like traditions. Probably the three most important elements are cheap lands, large crops and a pleasant winter climate."

While a few of this industrious people have for family reasons gone back to their former homes, nearly all are on their farms making substantial improvements, setting out orchards and raising vegetables in every month of the year. They also have good schools and churches established and both well supported. The Mennonites of Texas are already an important factor of the church, and during the past year they have received ministers and delegates from northern churches who are looking Texasward for other colony locations.

Brookshire A promising settlement has been started at Brookshire, thirty-five miles west of Houston, where good prairie lands may be obtained at prices varying from $5 to $8 an acre. About 6,500 acres have been secured. Hon. Fred. Harpster is in charge locally.

Fort Bend Colony *

The first colony located by the Mennonites was in Fort Bend County, seven miles south of Richmond and Rosenberg, on the Gulf, Colorado & Santa Fe Railway. Nearly 5,000 acres of black "hog-wallow" lands were bought for $10 per acre on favorable terms. More than forty families have already settled here and every week adds to their number. New houses have been built, the prairie broken, orchards planted, wells dug, and other improvements made. Schools, churches and store-buildings have been built and the success of the colony is assured.

During the twelve months succeeding the location of this colony many valuable improvements have been made. Farms of from 50 to 110 acres have been broken and planted to cotton, corn, vegetables, fruit, etc. Commodious houses have been erected and painted, and as every man's farm has both timber and water on the back end of it, and the residences are located centrally on Church and Concord Avenues, the scene in this thriving colony is an interesting one.

Fairbanks and Thompson *

The second Mennonite Colony was located at Fairbanks and Thompson Station, fourteen miles northwest of Houston in Harris County, on the Houston & Texas Central Railroad. A paved road is now completed from Houston nearly to Fairbanks, and will go beyond Thompson during the next year. This gives first-class facilities to drive with fruits and vegetables to a good market. Henry Lutkerman, a Kansas Mennonite, who came to Texas one year ago, has just completed a delivery of 450 bushels of sweet potatoes to the Houston market, raised on new ground. He also has a fine orchard started and has supported his family from other vegetables, eggs and chickens during his first year. He is enthusiastic over his prospects in his Southern home.

About 3,000 acres of good black-sandy loam lands have been purchased, and over forty families already located. It is expected that a hundred additional families will follow soon. Several thousand acres more can be secured when needed. Prices range from $4.50 to $7.50 per acre. This is prairie land, with plenty of timber.

Water is found at a depth of 15 to 30 feet. There is a fine road direct to the city of Houston. A saw mill and planing mill have been erected, and lumber can be obtained for $5 to $7 a thousand feet.

Westfield

The Westfield Colony was started by 115 persons who came in one party from Colorado. Members have since been received from several other states. The colony shows the effect of working together to a common end, for already extensive improvements have been made or are under way. Westfield is sixteen miles north of Houston, Harris County, on the International & Great Northern Railroad. A macadamized road connects the village with Houston. Several thousand acres of good black-sandy prairie land have been reserved, for sale at $5 to $6.50 per acre on terms to suit. Many of the old settlers in this locality are of German descent, having accumulated considerable of this world's goods. Schools and churches are within easy access. Rev. Henry Bergthold is the local agent.

HOUSTON HIGH SCHOOL.

Testimony of Farmers

• • •

It is one thing to generalize; quite a different affair to state particular facts. One may fluently speak in an impersonal way and general terms of the glorious empire state of Texas. Such adjectives may mean much or little. To prepare a statement of what has been accomplished on your own tract of land, with conclusions drawn from personal experience, requires scientific accuracy. An imaginative discourse will not pass muster.

Bearing this in mind, and in order that the situation in Texas might be fairly presented to outsiders, we have asked several farmers and fruit-raisers to tell herein their own story of success or failure, for the guidance of others. What they say, follows:

Rev. Henry Bergthold Rev. Henry Bergthold, of Westfield, Texas, formerly of Colorado, is evidently well pleased with his Texas venture, as may be seen from the following letter written by him in 1898:

"I came here from Colorado, and was a member of the first committee sent out to locate Mennonite colonies. My report being favorable a large party of us left Colorado and settled here. I had been in several Western States looking for a location and felt the great responsibility in selecting a home for my family and friends. We are now in Harris County, Texas, 16 miles north of Houston, which is our market. Although having settled here only a few months ago, we are doing what we started out to do—getting homes. Lumber being cheap, we soon had our houses built. Now we are breaking prairie and planting our gardens and orchards.

"I never saw a country where people can live so cheaply as soon as they get started. We have German neighbors here who have got a better start in one year than they could in five years in Colorado.

"Not for a single moment have I ever regretted coming to this Coast Country, and it looks now as though we, and those of our people who are now coming to the Westfield colony, would all own lands and homes of our own in a short time."

Rev. Bergthold reports, after a year's trial, that he is in good health and very hopeful for the future.

R. H. Bushway

Mr. R. H. Bushway, of Alvin, Texas, contributes the following statement, under date of January 13, 1898: " My native state is Illinois. I came to the Coast Country of Texas six years ago, since which time I have been continuously identified with the fruit industry. For the last four years my time has been devoted to the nursery business as founder and manager of the Alvin Nursery Co. Our grounds occupy forty acres of land, situated two and one-half miles from the city of Alvin. . Ten acres of this land is in bearing pear orchard, ten acres in an orchard two years old, and twenty acres now being put into cultivation. Besides the above, we have fourteen acres under lease, mostly planted in strawberries and nursery stock. Aside from the nursery our only commercial crop is strawberries, which have proven extremely profitable when properly grown and marketed.

" The following statement taken from our books for 1896 shows results obtained:

```
Number of 24-quart crates shipped from 7 acres...512
Total receipts...................................$1,217.00
Cost of 572 crates, at 18c..............$ 92.16
Cost of picking, at 60c. per crate ... 309.60
Nails, expenses, labor, etc........... 20.00      421.76
     Net proceeds of 7 acres................$  795.24
```

" Our berries are grown on black land without fertilizer of any kind, and by the system employed one man and team can plant and attend fifteen acres. By good cultivation and liberal application of commercial fertilizers, the above results can be increased threefold.

" In our six years' experience we have never had a crop failure, and only once a partial failure—even then good strawberry beds net their owners nearly $100 per acre. Such land as our berries are grown on can be bought in ten-acre blocks at from $15 to $30 per acre.

" While a large quantity of our products find a ready sale at good prices in the state, by far the greater percentage is shipped direct to the North, where the demand for our early berries and vegetables is only limited by our ability to produce. Almost our entire crop is shipped by express; however we that it will warrant a through freight service to such important points as Chicago, St. Louis and Kansas City, thereby reducing the cost of transportation to a minimum. We have been very successful in obtaining fancy prices for our early berries from northern markets and consider this outlet for our products practically unlimited, as we are fully three weeks earlier than our competitors.

"After six years of practical experience we have no hesitancy in affirming that every dollar intelligently invested in fruit growing in the Texas Coast Country will return three times the interest of the same amount invested in cotton or grain farming, proportionately to the capital put in.

" In regard to health will say that I came here badly affected with nasal catarrh and at the end of three years every symptom was gone, and nowhere does the general health appear so good.

" To the intelligent, industrious man or woman seeking to better their condition and acquire a home, the Texas Coast Country offers inducements not equalled by any other section—and to such is accorded a hearty welcome."

Under date of May 18, 1899, Mr. Bushway contributes the following additional data :

"The season just past has been the most prosperous financially that I have experiencèd during my seven years' residence in Alvin. As manager of the Alvin Nursery Company I am brought into personal contact with every section of what is properly known as the Gulf Coast Country, and especially am I familiar with that section adjacent to the Gulf, Colorado & Santa Fe Railway. Through increased production, not only have our people been able to secure a lower rate and better service, but the high quality of our goods has attracted buyers from all of the principal cities of the North. This has resulted in the sale of our produce at the depot, and eliminated the element of risk subsequent on consignment shipments.

"The sums realized this spring from some of our fruit and truck farms has been so large as to seem almost incredible. To cite a case in point, I refer to the experience of Mr. Otto Hoefs, a farmer living four miles south of Alvin. Up to April 25th he had realized from five acres of strawberries $1,690, and the season not nearly over. For six consecutive days he sold for cash on the streets of

A HILL OF STRAWBERRIES IN MARCH.

Alvin from this patch over $100 worth of berries per day. This is only one case; similar results from the same crop and also from other crops are common.

"Just at present every indication points to a rapid growth in population and an early advance in the price of land. While to-day the finest kind of land may be obtained at from $10 to $50 per acre, depending on location, this cannot last long, as the eyes of the homeseeker, the speculator and the investor have been attracted to the Coast Country. A case in point is that of the American Pear Company. Organized under the laws of Missouri and incorporated with a capital of $32,000, they have purchased a section of land close to Alvin of the Santa Fe Land and Improvement Company, and are planting the entire tract to Le Conte and Keiffer pears. Ten thousand trees are already set and growing, and the balance, 43,000 will be set this coming winter.

"Mr. W. E. Wagoman, president and general manager, is a thorough orchardist, having had years of practical experience in California. Mr. Wagoman, upon his first trip to the Coast Country, easily detected the superior advantages we possess of a low rate and short haul to the great markets of the United States.

"Another party now in Alvin is looking for a section of land to plant pears."

franz Heinrichs   Mr. Heinrichs visited the Coast Country several times and assisted in locating the first three colonies. He is a representative Mennonite; has bought and is improving 310 acres of land in the Fort Bend Colony; prefers South Texas to Kansas, because he finds here copious rainfall, no blizzards, scarcely any winter, a healthy climate and pure water.

"I think it is a good place for poor people," writes Mr. Heinrichs, "as vegetables can be raised every month in the year and the cattle and sheep business pays well, with free range.

"A friend of mine who came here from South Dakota with weak lungs is now well. He could not walk a quarter of a mile up north, but took a stroll of three miles here with me last month.

"With good markets and low-priced land, close to deep water ports at Houston and Galveston, we are bound to make money. Our Mennonite people like this country and more are coming."

The author of the above letter has to show for his first year's work three houses on a 300 acre farm in Ft. Bend Colony, of which more than 100 acres are under plow. He is closing out his Kansas farms to invest in sunny Texas.

Jesse W. Hill   "I came to Texas from middle Tennessee," writes Mr. Jesse W. Hill, of Arcola, Tex. "My farm is situated two and one-half miles northeast of Arcola. It consists of 160 acres of black-sandy and black-waxy soil. The line of the Gulf, Colorado & Santa Fe Ry. is two miles away. Eighty-five acres are in cotton, corn, oats, potatoes and strawberries, with a little corn and peanuts. Cotton is the staple crop, although potatoes, oats and strawberries do well. I have three or four hundred fruit trees, all growing. Had a partial failure once with corn, account drouth.

"By economy some profit can be realized. Markets are fairly good. I can sell everything I raise at living prices. Have not shipped any vegetables. The general health of the country is good. My family has had comparatively little sickness. Our health has been better here than for fifteen years past in other localities. Capacity for work is almost unlimited. I would recommend our country to any man who has enough means to improve his farm and pay expenses for a year."

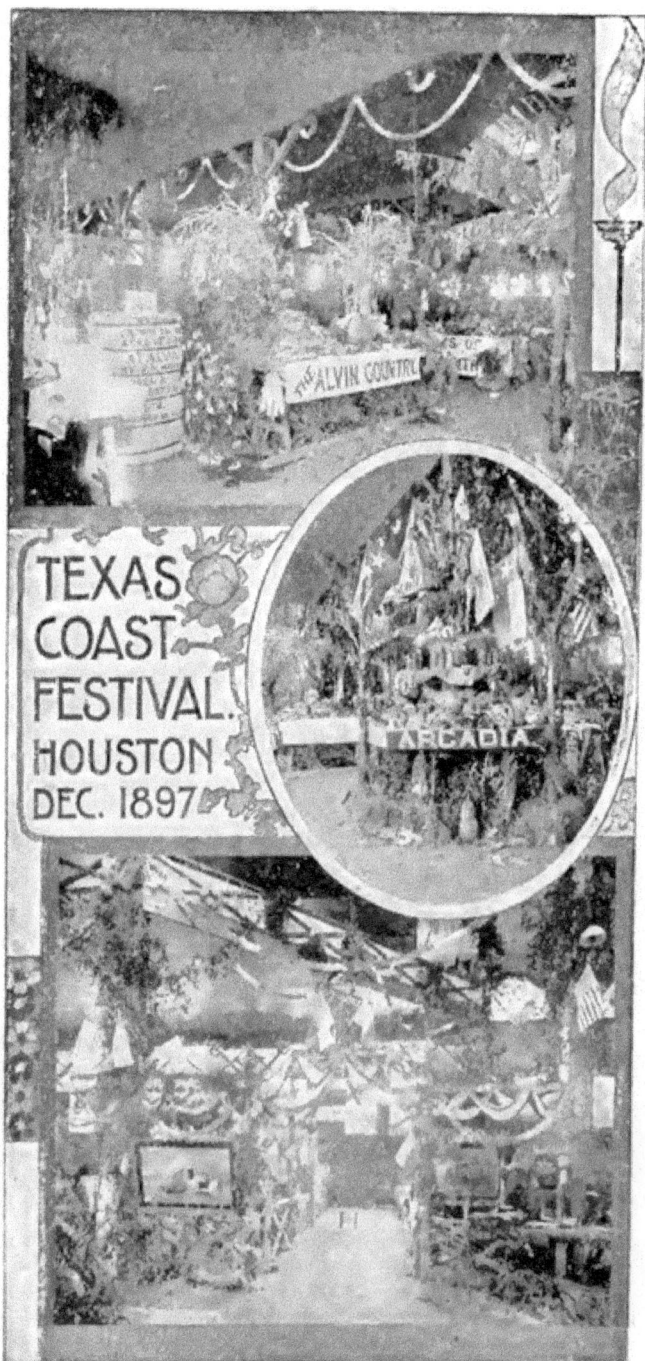

TEXAS COAST FESTIVAL ASSOCIATION, HOUSTON.

Jno. P. Klaassen The following letter is from Mr. Jno. P. Klaassen, once a resident of Lehigh, Kansas, now living in Texas. He was one of the committee appointed by the Mennonites to locate their Texas colonies and has carefully inspected the Coast Country. Mr. Klaassen says:

"I was one of the Committee of Eleven that located the first three colonies in Texas and am sure I did the best work of my life in starting a movement of our Mennonite people in this direction. Several of our committee visited and inspected the Coast Country, and in September, 1897, we located the first three colonies.

"December 18, 1897, I brought my family and a car of goods over the Santa Fe Route to my 300-acre place in the Fort Bend Colony; this was thirty days ago, and already I have erected a house, two sheds and chicken-houses, have 160 acres fenced-in, two wells dug (30 feet deep each), 40 acres broken and am ready to put out an orchard and garden; will break this year 100 acres more.

"Horses, mules, young cattle and sheep all do well here, but it is not best to bring old cows. We have good health. My wife and children are pleased —no more drouths and blizzards for us.

"I am glad that this movement of our people to Texas is taking such a wide range, covering not only the northwestern states, but Oregon and Manitoba, and recent correspondence from Russia goes to show that it is becoming a matter of interest in other countries as well—but there is plenty of room in Texas and cheap lands; let them come."

Mr. Klaassen has tried Texas one year since the above was written. He has a large neatly painted two-story house, barns, wells, orchard, and 150 acres plowed up. Write to him at Richmond, Texas, for his opinion of the Coast Country.

Eli Landreth Mr. Eli Landreth resides a quarter of a mile from Pearland station. He came to Texas from Iowa two years ago. His farm is a large one, consisting of 260 acres. Ninety acres are in cultivation, the main crops being oats, cotton, corn and sweet potatoes. Mr. Landreth reports that his crop of oats is more valuable than any other crop, while sweet potatoes exceed the others in quantity raised. He has not had much experience with fruit. Mr. Landreth is fortunate in being able to say that he has never had either a partial or complete failure of any crop, which perhaps accounts for the fact that averaging one year with another, his farm has paid a good profit on the investment.

In common with other residents of the Coast Country, he finds that school and church privileges and social advantages are all that could be desired, while the cost of living is cheaper than in the northern states.

The home market consumes the entire product of his land, and prices, as a rule, are good.

To quote Mr. Landreth: " I consider Southern Texas a very healthy country. Myself and family have enjoyed better health since coming here than for a number of years in Iowa. Had throat trouble in Iowa and am almost free from it now. Would recommend this section for persons of small means if they are willing to hustle. The chances of acquiring a competence with limited capital are far better than in any of the northern states."

E. Leming Mr. E. Leming is one of the small landowners at Alta Loma, Tex., coming here from Nebraska two years ago. His fourteen acres of ground is one-quarter of a mile from the station. Twelve acres are under cultivation; about one-half set to trees and grape vines, with an acre of asparagus. His orchard has not begun to bear yet. Mr. Leming reports that a slight freeze damaged his cauliflowers last November, otherwise crops have been successful. So far his little farm has not become a dividend producer; but he makes a living off of it. Taxes reasonable; schools fair. Home market does not consume all that he raises. Has shipped long distances by express and sold at good prices, but profits were considerably reduced by the transportation charges. Shipments by freight were a losing venture.

The general health of Mr. Leming has improved since coming to Alta Loma, and he can work with more comfort than in the North, except for a few days in midsummer, when the wind blows off the land. Finally, Mr. Leming advises that new settlers coming here should bring with them enough means to keep them for a year or two until the land can be brought into a proper state of cultivation.

O. P. Martin The 518-acre ranch of Mr. O. P. Martin, four miles from Pearland, has not yet been entirely opened up to cultivation. He now has 80 acres planted to cotton, corn, potatoes, peanuts and garden truck. Oats and hay are his most valuable crops. Mr. Martin has not yet engaged in fruitraising, has never had a failure and his products always yield a fair profit. He finds good local demand for everything he wishes to market.

".A person of small means," writes Mr. Martin, "can secure a home in this section easier than any other place I know of. Have never had better health than since coming to Pearland. With a family of seven, have not had any need for a doctor in four years. For a fine climate and pleasant home it can't be beat. Have never regretted leaving the snow banks of old Iowa for this ideal section of the sunny South."

A CAPE JESSAMINE FIELD OF TWENTY ACRES.

Aaron Peters Mr. Aaron Peters, of Fort Bend, Tex., a member of the Mennonite Church from South Dakota, bought 205 acres of good land at $10 an acre in the Fort Bend Colony. Each 100-acre tract has timber and water on the back end of it. He has already built a house and stable, at less than half what they would cost in Dakota. He has plowed his lands for trees and has a nice orchard set out.

Mr. Peters' family has had good health since coming to Texas nineteen months ago, and a great many of his old friends and neighbors are coming down this year to share the pleasant climate with him. He occasionally takes a trip over the Santa Fe to his former home in South Dakota to tell his friends how much better sunshiny Texas is with its mild winters. He pertinently inquires why his Mennonite brethren should stay north, where what is raised during one-half of the year is used in feeding for the other half.

S. N. Richardson Mr. S. N. Richardson came to Alvin, Texas, from North Carolina eighteen years ago, being one of the first settlers on an unbroken prairie, without a house in sight from Galveston to the Brazos, except a small settlement at Hitchcock. He owns twenty acres of sandy loam land within two blocks of the Gulf, Colorado & Santa Fe depot at Alvin. He raises pears, strawberries, peaches, plums and other fruits, flowers, corn, oats, garden vegetables and nursery stock. Pears, after they begin to bear well, are his best crop, running 500 bushels to the acre and increasing in quantity after the trees are eight years old; average price to date more than a dollar per bushel net. Cape jessamine flowers and plants are also leaders with him and pay well. Can grow 40 to 50 bushels of corn to the acre, and vegetables *ad libitum*.

He was one of the first to put cape jessamine flowers on sale; from small beginnings a few years ago this business has grown until the fragrant buds now bring in thousands of dollars yearly to growers; Maj. G. W. Durant is the largest jessamine grower at Alvin and perhaps in the United States, having twelve acres with daily output often exceeding 40,000 buds, which sell at 50 cents per hundred.

Mr. Richardson's pear orchard is twelve years old, and he has had no trouble thus far in disposing of product. Has also grown strawberries since 1882, with fine returns, crops being sure and sale certain, yielding $150 to $500 an acre. Peaches and plums have not been so profitable. Grapes have yielded fair returns. He thinks the Japan persimmon and fig are the coming fruits of this section. There has never been a complete failure, and never less than half a crop has been harvested. Blackberries and dewberries do well.

Prices of vegetables depend on the time of marketing. By getting in early, satisfactory prices may be realized. Crops must be planted to mature before competition of interior points is felt. If a man is awake to opportunities and takes advantage of them, he will make money—anywhere from $50 to $150 per acre. Planting season lasts for the whole year. Cabbages, beans, peas and tomatoes are the leading crops, followed by Irish potatoes and sweet potatoes. There is a succession of orchard, garden and field crops from January to December. State and county taxes are $1.10 per $100 valuation. School and church privileges are good. Alvin and the adjoining country neighborhoods have excellent educational and religious facilities.

The home market takes some produce, but bulk of it is shipped north. Mr. Richardson says he has shipped fruit and vegetables as far as Chicago and Denver by express with good success. Shippers are now mostly using fast freight in carload lots. He thinks a foreign market for fresh pears will soon be a necessity, unless facilities are afforded for evaporating or otherwise disposing of the large product.

"I came here for health," says this gentleman, "and have had it. There is no climatic disease and a man can work the year round. Strangers do not have to become acclimated, being as free from sickness as the old settlers. Persons suffering with lung and throat troubles are either greatly benefited or cured. This is a fine country for a rustler, but a lazy man is not at home here, for to succeed at the truck and fruit business requires energy and brains. Many men of small means have settled here and succeeded and there is room for more. I am satisfied that this is the best portion of the South. Here men with small capital can soon acquire a competence by industry combined with good judgment."

W. H. Thomas

Mr. W. H. Thomas, of Alta Loma, Tex., owns one of the largest farms in the vicinity, consisting of over 50 acres sandy loam. He came from Colorado three years ago and located one mile southeast of Alta Loma. Forty-five acres are under cultivation and set to an orchard of pears and plums, with some grapes. The best crop in quantity is sweet potatoes; in value, corn and peanuts.

Mr. Thomas has not raised much fruit as yet.

While there has been a partial failure in some of the crops, it was not complete. Prices are fair, and he is satisfied with his investment so far. Home market does not consume all that can be raised. Shipments of vegetables to Colorado have brought moderate returns, with better prospects for the future.

"I think the climate here in the Coast Country is No. 1," says Mr. Thomas. "Have found nothing to prevent one from continuous work. Further, I believe that settlers with funds enough to get a start, can with industry do very well here, providing their home experience has been along the line of raising small fruits and vegetables."

L. D. Troyer The following interesting letter from Mr. L. D. Troyer, of Fairbanks, Tex., a member of the Mennonite church, formerly of Missouri, but for over two years a resi- of Harris County, gives briefly his experience in the Coast Country, and his reasons for leaving the North. The communication is dated January 11, 1898:

"I removed from Cedar County, Mo. to the Coast Country of Texas, for the reason that my wife was told by her physicians that she must seek a better climate, or die. I also had been afflicted with catarrh for several years. We came to this Coast Country two years and a half ago. Today my wife is a well woman and I am entirely cured of catarrh. No money could induce us to go back to the North to live, as the climate, good health and a new prosperous country, growing rapidly, holds out great inducements to me.

"I want to say that this healthy climate, with its ocean breezes, and the good water found everywhere, has given us both a new lease of life, and several of my neighbors have come here and are equally well pleased.

"The Mennonites, who have already located five colonies in the vicinity of Houston, have made no mistake in this removal, nor in

STEM OF KEIFER PEARS.

COTTON EXCHANGE, HOUSTON.

selecting the Santa Fe as the official route. With the deep water ports just opened, and immigration from the North steadily increasing, the good lands and rich soil of South Texas will make our industrious, Mennonite church people, not only a good living, but a competence, and at the prices land has been bought for them there it hardly a question but that it will double in value within the next two years Their investments here in lands are so much less, while their profits are so much greater (on account of being near markets and deep water ports) than in the North, that they will continue to be as they now are, entirely satisfied with the change.

" Another point which I deem important: Vegetables, melons, fruits, as well as grains, (all of which do well here) should be shipped in carload lots, and our people grouped together as they are, can arrange to plant so as to ship in that way and receive the largest amount of profits from their labors. They can raise in the late fall onions, cabbage, celery, potatoes, cauliflower and other vegetables, so as to ship them North in carloads early in the spring, where they will find a bare market. Then, in the late summer, another crop for the late winter shipment to the North. In this way they will make it extremely profitable. Our Mennonite people will raise a large acreage of melons this year on the sod.

" These dark sandy loam lands around the city of Houston, are rapidly being settled up, and I can assure my Mennonite friends of a warm welcome."

71

WAY DOWN SOUTH IN THE LAND OF COTTON

Pear Orchards

• • •

SUCH is the importance of the pear industry of the Gulf Coast of Texas, that a special article is devoted to that topic.

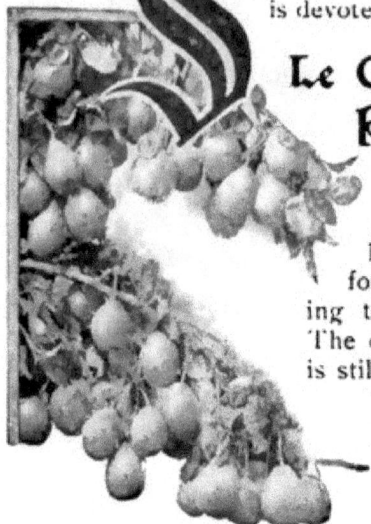

Le Conte Pear The Le Conte Pear is supposed to be an American seedling from the ancestral Asiatic pear, which, in its own home, is an immense forest tree, often attaining the age of 300 years. The original Le Conte tree is still standing in Georgia, a magnificent specimen, hardy, beautiful and prolific. These wonderful new pears are as hardy as forest trees, of luxuriant foliage, grow to a great size, are here free from blight, and yield every year an enormous crop of fruit which sells in Eastern and Northern markets at prices that compete with the older and better known varieties. As a fruit for canning, drying or preserving, they are acknowledged as unequaled. When picked somewhat green and ripened in cellars, many connoisseurs pronounce them equal to the famous Bartlett.

The Le Conte of the Coast Country is the earliest pear grown anywhere in the United States. It can be placed upon the market during the latter part of June, which is fully three weeks earlier than fruit can be plucked in California. The Le Conte is a very fair eating pear; while it does not rank as high as some varieties or command the highest prices, it is a pear that supplies the market, patronized by the middle class. The Le Conte is a very rapid grower, and yields abundantly; in fact it is subject

73

to over production, which must be guarded against. More than 9,000 bushels of Le Conte pears were shipped from thirteen acres of nine and ten year old trees in H. M. Stringfellow's orchard at Hitchcock, during 1893, and the subsequent product has been marketed in equally large quantities.

A Coast Country orchard of Le Conte and Keifer pear trees, upward of ten years of age, properly attended to, should yield a certain annual revenue of $300 to $500 per acre above all expense of taking care of the trees and cost of marketing the fruit.

J. J. SHIRLEY'S PEAR ORCHARD, ALVIN.

Other Varieties On the Gulf Coast of Texas there has rarely been a failure of the Le Conte, Keifer and Garber pear crop, while in quality the fruit grown in more northern climes suffers in comparison. The Keifer is grown for home consumption. The Garber is better adapted for shipment.

Mr. J. J. Shirley, of Alvin, reports that about 70 to 100 trees are set to the acre, and at ten years old they produce 5 to 10 bushels of pears to the tree. He has one Keifer tree ten years of age, which last season yielded 17 bushels, worth $20; also one Le Conte tree at ten years yielded 16 bushels, for which he got $15. These were his best trees, and should not be taken as a standard by which to estimate average proceeds. In 1897

Texas buyers paid $1 per bushel for the pears, boxed and put into the cars at the point of shipment.

Mr. Sampson, near Alvin, has 23,000 pear trees, and many orchards run from 2,000 to 10,000. The Garbers ripen shortly after the Le Contes are through bearing, say early in August. After the Garbers the Keifers begin to ripen, between September 1st and 10th and continue to bear until about the middle of October. The Garber ranks as one of the choicest of eating pears. The Keifer is best suited for canning and preserving. Other varieties grown are the Bartlett and Smith's Hybrid. A few years will find whole train loads of pears being shipped north. At present quite heavy sales are made in Northern Texas, Indian Territory, Kansas and Nebraska. From $1 to $1.25 per bushel is realized.

Texas pears may be canned, preserved, evaporated or made into cider and vinegar. The profits are certain and adequate.

The Profits That fruit culture pays is evidenced by the following statement of profits realized by owners of pear orchards in the vicinity of Alvin. The figures are gleaned from an article published in a local paper at that point during 1898.

The Boher orchard of twelve acres (poor improvements but first-class trees) was bought by Mr. Lawler over two years ago for $5,000, and last fall Mr. Lawler sold it to Mr. Haley for $7,000. Mr. Boher paid $12.50 per acre for the land and only cultivated it four years. In that period he made expenses from vegetables grown between the tree rows. The $5,000, less $150, was clear money.

"Fairy Land," owned by Mr. McDonald, 40 acres, only about half in orchard, sold two years ago for $12,000.

Dr. Fehrenkamp paid $8,000 for 51 acres adjoining Major Durant's.

The John F. Durant place of 35 acres sold a year ago for $7,500.

The Nesbit orchard of 20 acres sold three years ago for $3,250.

The Zychlinski orchard of 36 acres was purchased for $5,000.

Mr. E. D. Carter paid $2,250 for his orchard of four and one-half acres.

Prof. J. J. Shirley bought 50 acres twelve years

ago for $6 per acre and refused $16,000 for his orchard over two years ago. He has a large family and they have made a living from the vegetables, strawberries, etc., grown on the place.

Mr. Henry Sampson has 163 acres which he purchased some six years ago for about $10 per acre. On this he has 19,000 pear trees besides other fruits. He says he would not take a cent less than $40,000 for his orchard.

Mr. G. H. Cook has 26 acres, on which he has been living some ten years, and besides growing one of the finest orch-

GATHERING PEARS AT ALVIN.

ards in this section he has made money and a name as one of the most successful strawberry growers. He refused $6,000 three years ago for his place.

The editor concludes by saying: " If you would establish an orchard and do not wish to do the work yourself, all that is necessary is to buy the land (say 20 acres) at $25 per acre—which would be $500. Expense of plowing same will be $50; fencing, $75; buying and planting 2,000 pear trees, $200. Here we have an outlay of $825, or half as much for ten acres. After this is done, there are plenty of good men who will contract to take the land and care for the orchard for what they can make on it."

There's Money in Strawberries

● ● ●

Year by year the acreage of strawberries in the Coast Country has been increased until now that luscious berry contributes a large share toward the fruit grower's income. The growing of this berry for market rivals in profit the culture of the pear, and the acreage is steadily increasing. It brings in a fair return the first year after planting. You don't get gray-haired waiting

IN A FIELD OF STRAWBERRIES, MARCH 5TH.

for results. Beginning with raw prairie, an acre of strawberries will have cost, to break, harrow, plant, fertilize and cultivate, about $70. The net return next year should not be less than $200, and the same each of the following years. The best results are secured by resetting plants annually.

A prominent grower of strawberries at Alvin states that during March, 1898, he and his three boys picked from one-eighth of an acre seven and a half twenty-four quart crates of strawberries and shipped them to Denver, where they sold for $8 per case, which was $60 for the lot. This was new land and the first crop off of it.

So important a position has this product assumed that more extended mention than heretofore can properly be given it.

The country around Alvin has some of the biggest strawberry patches in the country. Inquiries recently addressed to prominent growers in that locality have elicited the following interesting replies:

By Otto Hoefs "I have had three acres in cultivation in strawberries this year of the improved Mitchell variety. These berries were grown on black sandy soil well cultivated and mulched with light coating of prairie hay in January. I sold a part of them on the Alvin market and a part I shipped to Kansas City and other markets. I realized from these three acres $1,700. I also had a three acre patch of new plants put in late in the fall and from these three acres I realized $365."

By Wm. A. Dennis "I have six acres in strawberries, but about one acre was set to berries late last fall and did not produce any to speak of, so that my crop was gathered from five acres. Am cultivating the Hoffman variety principally, although I had one-third acre of the Lady Thompson berry, from which I have netted almost $200, or at the rate of $600 per acre and consider it one of the most profitable varieties. I have shipped up to date 312 crates, net $960, or an average of $3.10 per crate. Consider the strawberry crop one of the most valuable that can be raised in the Coast Country and will give it almost our entire attention hereafter."

By W. H. Miller "I have three acres of strawberries—half Hoffman, half Mitchel; use no fertilizer. Sold 400 crates of 24 quarts each at $2.52 per crate. Deducting expense of packing and picking and the net result was $1.80 per crate or $720 for the three acres. Receipts would have averaged fifty cents a crate more but for a few mismanaged shipments to outside points. Demand by home buyers active and their prices remunerative. Strawberries are a sure crop with proper care; they come in earlier here than farther north and last longer. I can make more money with less labor on three acres of strawberries than on one hundred of cotton in any country. This is a great country for the poor man."

By W. H. Rogers "We have sold up to date (May 21, 1899) off one acre of Hoffman strawberries and one and a half acres of Rogers dewberry, 330 crates at an average of $2.70 per crate net. The Hoffman and Michel are the two leaders in strawberries, but the Rogers dewberry and the Dallas blackberry are both money makers and should have a place on every farm in the Coast Country. We are still picking from six to ten crates daily, which net us $1.75 per crate. This beats four cent cotton. The berry crop is the money crop here, still we can raise fine vegetables and get fair prices for them. The fact that the growers could sell their berries and vegetables for cash in hand at Alvin has been worth at least twenty-five per cent to the farmers of this vicinity."

By W. W. Ware "From my seven-eighths of an acre in strawberries of the Hoffman variety I gathered 182½ crates, which brought in $564.80. I think this berry is a good paying crop, and it can be depended upon, too."

By C. W. Benson "Most of my new planting of berries was of the Newman variety and the freeze in February hurt the plants. Cannot exactly tell what the total returns were from the best field, as we picked from two acres of old beds which were run out, but the gross receipts were much more than we expected and prices ruled very firm, averaging fully $3 per crate net for the season. The Hoffman berry has proved to be very remunerative here—perhaps the best, but it may be closely followed by Lady Thompson in future seasons—I shall extend my berry acreage this year wholly in the two varieties named. About seventy-five per cent of the sales at Alvin prior to May 1st were for cash, and many days the entire pick was sold on the streets. The future of the strawberry as a money crop for this section appears to be merely a matter of quality. Good fruit will always be in demand in March and April and we have practically no competition for a period of sixty days."

By H. R. Dietrich "Can strawberries and vegetables be grown here with profit? I believe Alvin and the Coast Country to be the best region in Texas or the United States for berry culture. Eight years ago I came with my family from Galveston, never having had any experience whatever in farming, having been seven years in the commission business. This year I had four acres in berries, two and one-half acres in early Mitchell, one-half acre in Hoffman and one acre in Norman. The first two varieties did well. In all I sold $1,014 worth. As soon as the price got down too low I stopped selling and made preserves and wine out of my berries, for which latter there is always a cash market. The last six years I made from $75 to $350 per acre from my berries. One of my neighbors sold this season over $600 of berries from one and one-quarter acres. I have made from my berries from $500 to $1,300 a year. If I had the experience eight years ago that I have now I would probably be $3,000 better off financially. I see no reason why I cannot make $1,500 to $3,000 per year in the culture of strawberries in the Alvin country."

STRAWBERRIES PICKED ON CHRISTMAS DAY.

Miscellaneous Products

• • •

Grapes Grapes are planted, cultivated and marketed on the Texas Coast just as they are in California, except that the vineyards of Texas bear no comparison in area with the great grape-growing regions of the Pacific Coast.

Enough has been done from which to form an opinion as to the profitableness of the industry. Leading horticulturists declare that a Texas vineyard, intelligently located and planted with the right varieties, is a certain source of wealth.

The following grapes grow here in a perfection that no country on earth can excel: Chasselas Muscat or Muscatelli, Chasselas Rose de Peru, Emperor, Black Morocco or Tokay (both flame and white), Malaga or Chasselas Napoleon, Black Spanish, Lenoir or Black Burgundy, Goethe, Rogers No. 1, Salem, Rogers No. 53, Niagara, Black July, Roulander, Delaware, Missouri, Rissling and Herbemont.

If well fertilized, most varieties come into bearing the second year, and when three years old may be counted on for a yield of ten to fifteen pounds of luscious grapes to the vine, and much more as they increase in age.

The Herbemont, Black Spanish and Niagara have proven themselves to be the most successful, as much as $200 net having frequently been obtained from two acres of Niagaras from one crop. The common American varieties all succeed here.

Vegetables The cauliflower will, in the near future, be raised in large quantities for shipment in carload lots. A salt atmosphere seems to be essential to the perfect development of this vegetable, and as the soil here is well adapted to it, every condition is favorable to its growth. It is strictly a fall vegetable, and when sown early in July, and set out in August in rich soil, the bulk of the crop can be marketed before January.

Cabbages, when planted at the right time, yield large returns. There is scarcely a limit to the quantities that can be disposed of in the Northwest.

FIG ORCHARD AND RAMIE FIELD. ONE YEAR OLD. AT CLEAR CREEK.

when grown in sufficient numbers to warrant carload shipments. Big crops are raised at Bolivar Point.

The Creole and White Queen onions are as successfully grown here as near New Orleans. They mature in April when northern onions are sprouting, and the demand is unlimited at $1 per bushel.

It is demonstrated that the tomato will produce abundantly in the Coast Country. It begins to ripen May 20th, and at once finds ready sale at high prices all over Texas.

Irish potatoes do well everywhere; the early planting rarely brings under seventy-five cents a bushel in season. Beans, cucumbers, squashes and watermelons are grown in limited quantities.

Rice Southeast Texas is fully equal to southwest Louisiana for rice growing. Upwards of 30,000 acres were sown last season, the output being worth $1,250,000.

To insure a good rice crop, two factors are essential: a level body of land, and an abundance of water. In Louisiana water is largely supplied by pumping from water courses with steam pumps. On the Texas coast it can be had from artesian wells at no cost other than the boring of the well.

To plant an acre of rice the first time will cost $15 This includes fences, ditches, levees, plowing and, planting. After the ground is once prepared, subsequent planting may be done for $8 per acre. Planting season is from latter part of April to last of June, and crop is ready for harvest in five months from time of planting, thus furnishing ready money while waiting for other crops to mature. It is planted, harvested and threshed very much the same as wheat and at the same expense, and yields from twelve to eighteen barrels of rough rice per acre, worth an average of $3.50 per barrel.

A prominent rice planter of Liberty, Texas, reports receipts of $3,700 from eighty acres in 1893. and the entire expense only $500, a net profit of $27.50 per acre. If the rice straw is compressed into bales, and sold for feed, it will pay the cost of the rice crop. Other products resultant from milling are rice bran and rice polish, the former making a nutritious feed for stock, while the latter resembles buckwheat flour.

Rice lands with water privileges may be rented at

one-fifth for water toll and one-fifth for land rent, leaving about $25 per acre net, or for the usual one hundred acre tract, $2,500 to the tenant.

This industry is now in its infancy in Texas, but the farmers, realizing that some valuable crop must take the place of cotton, which hitherto has been raised in too great abundance, are turning their attention to rice culture with much favor.

Some of the advantages of rice culture over wheat are: (1) The long period during which the ground can be prepared and the grain sown. Preparations can be carried on from October until June, sowing from March until July, and harvesting extends over a period of nearly four months, from August to November, inclusive; (2) the greater value of the product; (3) the yield per acre, which is from eight to twenty barrels of 162 pounds each.

A great deal of money can be made in a few years in rice cultivation. As the total amount of rice raised in the United States is about one-half the annual consumption, the output can be largely increased without danger of over-production. Another factor is the limited area remaining that can be planted to rice.

A FIELD OF SUGAR CANE.

Sugar Cane There is money in sugar cane. One million acres of south Texas land is suitable for its production. As a matter of fact, only 15,000 acres are devoted to this industry (a paltry percentage) and yet in 1895 the Texas sugar crop sold for $1,500,000, an average of nearly $100 per acre. Seventy dollars an acre may be reasonably counted on, one year with another, one acre of ground turning off 20 to 50 tons of cane, marketable at $3.00 a ton.

Hitherto it has taken a big capital to run a sugar plantation, because in addition to raising the cane it was necessary to change it into sugar in one's own mill. The man with a plow and a mule, however industrious and foresighted, was barred out for lack of dollars. Conditions are changing rapidly, and capitalists are now erecting large central sugar mills, similar to the central factory in Cuba and Louisiana. The small farmer takes his cane there and brings its value back immediately in cash. By this plan the farmer can grow ten acres or five hundred, and the owners of sugar lands can rent them to tenant farmers. The separation of cane growing and sugar-making processes is in line with the system of large packing houses that consume the steer and porker.

The annual expense for planting an acre of sugar-cane will not exceed $6 to $8, because planting is only necessary every third or fourth year. To cultivate cane is not half as expensive as to care for a field of cotton. The hardest part is the work of harvesting. Each individual stalk must be cut by hand, a process requiring time and labor.

Sugar is a remarkable crop in the amount of money it diffuses through labor. It requires much care, much handling and much machinery. It represents a large outlay and brings in a large profit.

Mr. J. H. House, owner of the Arcola Plantation, near Houston, says that his profit per acre per annum in cultivating sugar cane is $80, and that the crop is never failing, though some years it is larger than others.

At Sugarland Ed. H. Cunningham & Co. have one of the largest sugar refineries in the world. The plant represents an investment of nearly $1,000,000. This establishment not only refines sugar, but recently introduced a paper mill, the paper being made from the pulp of the sugar cane.

Cotton Everybody knows cotton is king, even in these times of tottering thrones; but everybody does not know that Texas produces from one-quarter to one-third of the crop grown in this country. The annual yield varies from two to three and a half million bales. Houston alone handles over half of the cotton crop of Texas.

The Texas cotton belt is divided by Nature into six districts. The territory along the coast, while not producing as many bales as the central district, excels it in the number of pounds raised to the acre. It used to be thought that cotton could not be produced on the open prairie lands. The prairies are equal to, if not superior to the river bottom sections, and the first cost of land is much less. The average yield is from three-quarters to a bale and a half of cotton to the acre. Prairie lands yield from a half to one bale per acre and bottom lands 50% more. Cotton varies in price from $25 to $45 per bale. Mr. W. T. Taylor, of Wharton, affirms that in spite of the dry weather of 1897 he raised 600 bales on 750 acres.

Cotton is the Coast Country farmer's monopoly. It is just as convertible into money as a nugget of gold. Owing to fertile soil, good climate and intelligent culture, this part of Texas combines maximum yield with minimum cost. The best results are reached on small farms, with home labor. Under such circumstances success is as nearly sure as sunrise. The Texas cotton raiser who puts brains into his business, does not have to wait until old age for a competency even with the low prices recently prevailing. The cotton planter finds here new land, splendidly adapted to his purpose. Another advantage is cheap labor. Mexican cotton pickers can be brought in, who will work reasonably and well.

It is thought that within the next few years the credit of being the first sea island cotton market of the world will be transferred from Charleston, S. C. to Galveston or Houston.

Another great source of profit is the use which cotton seed may be put to. Aside from the oil, nothing fattens cattle quicker than cotton seed meal and hulls.

Oranges Oranges do fairly well on the Texas Coast. It is expected that with the introduction of certain hardy varieties from Japan the orange will come to have an established commercial value as an article of export.

Figs Figs grow in the greatest profusion. Fruit-growers who are beginning to cultivate it claim it is the most profitable fruit that can be raised in this locality. Two hundred fig trees can be planted to the acre, which will begin to bear in two years and be in full bearing in five years, and will then yield annually 200 pounds of fruit each, a net profit, when dried and preserved, of $3 per tree.

STRAWBERRY FIELD IN THE DICKINSON COUNTRY.

Plums Texas is the home of the plum. It grows wild in the woods in luxuriant profusion. No less than three kinds of wild plums grow in southern Texas, all of fine quality and marketable. The Japan plum is a comparative failure. The American or Chickasaw variety is a success.

Poultry Any practical man can take ten acres of land, and 600 of the best laying hens, and by raising his own feed clear $1,000 to $1,500 each year, and have his fruit trees growing on the same ground. "Broilers" find a ready market in Houston at twenty-five to thirty-five cents a head.

Dairying The fact that milk retails in Houston at ten cents a quart and butter at twenty-five cents a pound, is enough to show that a practical dairyman, who raises his own feed, can realize fifty to seventy-five per cent. profit on his investment and not work very hard either.

Transportation The key to the whole problem here, as elsewhere, where a surplus can be produced, is a good, near-at-hand market, with quick transportation to foreign markets. The Gulf counties of Texas are everywhere accessible to Houston and Galveston by rail or water. Numerous streams and bayous are navigable inland for long distances by schooners and steamboats. Several hundred small schooners and steamers daily ply between Galveston and neighboring inland places, engaged in carrying freight. The Santa Fe Route opens up a vast market in north Texas, Oklahoma, Colorado, Kansas City, St. Louis and Chicago. But the best guarantee of good prices is the fact that everything here matures several weeks earlier than a hundred miles inland or anywhere else in the United States, except the south end of Florida and Louisiana. The first half of the crop can always be marketed without competition.

A Review and Outlook

• •

By Mr. Stringfellow

• •

Review It is just fifteen years since I moved to Hitchcock to embark in the fruit and vegetable business, and plant the first successful pear orchard in the Coast Country.

At that time the total number of residents along the Santa Fe line between Virginia Point and Alvin could have been counted on the two hands. The Houston branch had not been started; the Santa Fe had just crossed the Brazos River on its march to the North, and a single train up in the morning and down at night, constituted the entire service. Hitchcock was the only settlement between the bay and Houston.

It seems almost incredible that the short space of fifteen years could have sufficed for the wonderful development that has since taken place. Instead of creeping slowly over an open, wild prairie, and through herds of wandering long-horns at the rate of fifteen or twenty miles an hour, once a day, the traveler now speeds at three times that pace, and six times a day, each way, through an almost continuous succession of orchards and gardens on each side of the track, and hundreds of packages of fruit and vegetables daily leave the various bustling little towns along the road. This rapid change from the prairie-waste, with its sea of waving grass, to fertile fields and cozy homes, has been due almost entirely to the wise liberality and fostering care of the various managements, both freight and passenger, of the Santa Fe Railroad.

Of course, in its progress to the present high state of development, Coast Country settlers have had obstacles to overcome in places, and disappointments to bear here as well as elsewhere. Drouth, frost and excessive rains have occasionally worked serious harm; but the length of our seasons, and the great variety of products that can be grown, nearly always allow the growers to recoup themselves on a

89

different and successful crop in case one should from any cause be a failure.

Let us see how the Coast Country now stands (Spring of '97). From a few packages of vegetables and berries fifteen years ago, we are now growing and shipping thousands of crates annually, and best of all, have induced buyers from distant markets to send their agents down to purchase the various products on the ground. This is by far the most satisfactory plan.

As to the future of this section, there can be little doubt that it has advanced beyond the experimental stage. While lands have shrunk in value from the boom prices of ten years ago, they are now on a substantial and reasonable basis, below which they are never likely to fall. The bottom has been touched, and the present time affords opportunities that are not likely to remain long. But, while lands will hardly go lower in Galveston County, it will be folly to buy largely on credit, expecting to make a living and pay for it out of the ground at the same time. This has been a fatal mistake of many of the early settlers of this section. They came with insufficient means, inflated ideas of profits, and often lacked that real love for the business which is the greatest secret in successful fruit and vegetable growing; without it, losses and failure will quickly disgust the planter for money only, which the genuine lover of the business would have borne with patience and conquered by persevering efforts.

Prices of all fruits and vegetables have now come to bedrock all over the country, but if they can be grown with profit anywhere, it can be done here.

In addition to this, we have a most delightful and healthy climate, and the most progressive and liberal railroad in the country, and if a man has made up his mind to change his home (while, of course, it is a serious move) he should give the merits of the Coast Country of Texas a careful examination before taking the step.

The Outlook "Two years ago I wrote the above review and am glad to say that there has since been a steady improvement until there is now (early summer of 1899) a general confidence that the future is full of promise. There have been some failures on the part of individuals who were unsuited to rural life and without sufficient means to make a success, but such conditions always prevail in the development of all new countries. While the past winter has been exceptionally severe and the late freeze in February unparalleled in the history of this section, still the Coast Country of Texas has shown its remarkable resources and wonderful recuperative powers by turning out, in spite of these obstacles, one of the most profitable crops we have ever had. The strawberry has been particularly remunerative and with the increased acreage, both of berries and vegetables, have come buyers to take the output directly from the growers. With years of experience the people have now found out what crops are most profitable, as well as improved methods of growing them, and also learned to appreciate the importance of raising, as largely as possible, their feed stuffs at home. Corn, oats, sorghum, peanuts and cow peas are being generally planted and prairie hay saved in increasing quantities. Up to the severe freeze of February 15th the promise for an immense pear crop was never so good, but unfortunately the low temperature caught the sap in motion and caused a large part of the Le Conte to shed. The Keiffer, however, which blooms later, has all the fruit the trees can carry. The grapes were entirely unhurt and the prospects for a fine yield could not be better. The Niagara is most generally planted and has never yet made a failure. The interest in fig culture received a check from the killing to the ground of many of the tender varieties, though the Celeste, in most instances, came through all right. But the fig renews itself so quickly and bears so early, that even the loss of a tree means only the missing of one or two crops. Even the China and mulberry trees were killed in many places, a thing which never happened before nor is likely to occur again in many years. Taken altogether the outlook is very bright. While most of the states are locked up in ice and snow for months, our farmers and gardeners need lose scarcely a day except from rain, and enjoy a climate almost entirely exempt from pneumonia, diphtheria and typhoid fever, three of the worst diseases of the North. Lands are still very cheap but will advance in the near future.

H. M. STRINGFELLOW."

TYPICAL SCENES ON A SOUTHERN PLANTATION.

Crops
That Yield Money Quickly

• • •

Mr. C. W. Benson is local agent of Wells, Fargo & Co.'s Express at Alvin, Texas. His experience, both as a fruit grower and a handler of all kinds of products grown around Alvin, is sufficiently varied and practical to give his remarks more than ordinary force. Mr. Benson says:

"More should be written about what·has been done in money crops in the Coast Country. The writer came to Alvin five years ago without experience, bought 20 acres of land, has expended in improvements, including good residence and farm buildings, $3,000.

"Our receipts from the place in 1898 were $2,800; expenses $950. We have produced $500 from two acres of tomatoes, $200 per acre from four acres of strawberries ($550 from fruit plats and $250 from plant plats). One dollar and ten cents per hill was netted last spring on 83 hills of cucumbers in hotbed on our place.

"Only a small portion of the land has been producing. Three acres devoted to flowers gave us over $1,000. We will fruit for the first time this year, one acre of grapes, one acre of blackberries, and half an acre of peaches, and have maturing two acres of pears, one-half acre of dewberries, two acres of figs, one acre of nursery stock and five and one-half acres of vegetables (worked in unused spaces); also one-fourth acre of asparagus.

"To my positive knowledge grapes have paid over $100 per acre here; blackberries $125 per acre, and dewberries (estimated from small plats) $125; peaches were produced for the first time last season —much of the fruit was large enough to completely fill a coffee cup, and sold from 60c to 90c per one-third bushel net. Figs paid one of my neighbors $450 for three acres. Nursery stock pays from $150 to $300 per acre, but should, perhaps, have irrigation to make it safe. Vegetables pay from $35 to $75 per acre, including sweet potatoes, which netted the grower $8 per ton last fall. Winter vegetables were, of course, lost this spring in the February freeze, but when there are crops coming on ten months in the year it is less discouraging than where nothing but short seasons prevail.

"Touching on pears—it is quite probable that they will prove less remunerative than was at first supposed, and I consider it vitally important that true estimates should be given. Pear orchards already planted should pay fairly good returns, but diversification is now the order of the day.

"I share Mr. Stringfellow's opinion that certain varieties of oranges and also asparagus will prove to be two of our best paying crops, and many small experiments are now under way in both lines.

"Several cash buyers of fruit and vegetables are permanently located here, and the markets which look to us for their supply not only pay better prices than eastern markets, but at present are somewhat less discriminating or exacting as to certain standards in quality. This is an advantage to inexperienced growers until they can learn to produce and pack the various commodities in better grades and more attractive form."

CULTIVATING HORSE RADISH.

The
Diversified Interests of Texas

● ● ●

Extracts from an interview with Mr. Jas. A. Davis, Industrial Commissioner of the Santa Fe Route, which appeared in the *Chicago Daily Record* of March 14, 1898 :

"Texas, with its area of 270,000 square miles, is an empire richer in itself than Chicago and the West generally begin to appreciate. Within that area are greater diversities of products and more pursuits are possible than in a similar area in any part of the world. Cotton is, and will, of course, continue to be, the chief staple product. It is evident from last season's experience that cotton can be grown there more profitably than anywhere else. The wheat area is rapidly being enlarged, and many flouring mills are now operating in the state and using only Texas wheat. Tobacco is being successfully cultivated and additional lands are being used for this purpose. Sugar manufacturers, too, are finding practical and profitable possibilities in sugar lands in the southern portion of the state. The pine-timber interests are some of the largest in the country, the output for 1896 having aggregated 400,000,000 feet. For farmers Texas offers an exceedingly good field for the cultivation of small fruits.

" For high-grade wools Texas is considered by experts to be second only to Australia. Texas cattle are known all over the United States. Oil has been found in paying quantities, and there are indications of new coal fields.

" The manufacturing interests of the state are increasing and the field is now open to many new industries. The local conditions for such are exceptionally favorable, there being an abundance of raw materials close at hand. The average prosperity of the state is high. The farmers are all greatly encouraged and are engaged in studying the diversification of crops and the possibility of reducing the cost of raising cotton and wheat by giving attention to other farm products. There is a section of the country on the San Angelo branch of the Santa Fe where wheat and cotton are raised side by side on the same farm.

"The towns in Texas are growing rapidly. Galveston, Houston, Belton, Temple, Weatherford, Cleburne, Fort Worth, Dallas and Gainesville all show signs of increasing prosperity. The advantages of Galveston as a port are becoming better known every year, and it promises to be one of the leading ports in the country. Chicago and the west are considerably interested in the development of Galveston's port facilities, as in some measure offsetting any monopolistic tendencies on the part of the Atlantic ports."

PICKING BEANS ON CHADWICK'S PLACE.

Successful Tobacco Culture

• • •

The article below was contributed by Mr. W. B. Slosson, of the Houston Newcomers' Association, Houston, Texas, March 18, 1898:

" Please advise the world that the purest and best of Havana tobacco has been, and is now being grown, in at least six counties of the Coast Country. This innovation of transferring the raising of that high-priced staple to southeast Texas is of great interest to newcomers from the North.

" Last year 600 acres of this tobacco was raised. 1898 will see from 9,000 to 12,000 acres grown. The market price of ordinary tobacco is from seven to eleven cents per pound. The price paid to our Texas farmers for Havana tobacco was from fifty cents to one dollar per pound. The duty on Havana tobacco is $1.35 to $2.00 on wrappers, both of which can be raised and handled here as cheaply as common tobacco heretofore raised.

" On February 26, 1898, a meeting of the Texas Tobacco Growers' Association (A. R. P. Moore, of Houston, president) was held at the Houston Business League. At this meeting, Mr. S. J. Washburn, Vice-President of the DeWitt County Tobacco Growers' Association, said: 'We could dispose of 20,000 cars of this tobacco in a single season. There is no limit to the demand for fine cigar tobacco We have the climate and the soil to grow to advantage light tobacco from Havana seed, and in only a small portion of the United States can these grades be raised. New England and New York are nearly driven out of the market already, for the reason that we can grow better grades for less money.'

" Messrs. Mitchellson & Hubbard, of Kansas City, leaf tobacco dealers, offered me one dollar a pound for some specially high grades that I raised last year. Although I am familiar with tobacco-raising in Missouri, Wisconsin and Ohio, I am sure better profits can be had from raising it in southeast Texas than any other part of the Union.

" Owen Smith & Co., of southeast Texas, sold their crop of 60,000 pounds at sixty cents a pound.

T. J. Rountree produced, last year, 13.000 pounds from eighteen acres, selling 10,000 pounds at fifty cents and the remainder at twenty-five cents.

"The absence of severe winds here is a large factor in tobacco culture. The cheap lands, the high duties on imported tobacco, the long seasons, a large rainfall and an equable climate, makes this Coast Country of Texas especially attractive to settlers who desire to diversify their crops.

"In a state like Texas, where nearly all the staple grains are raised successfully (a state which also raises *one-third* of the whole cotton crop of America), where *all* the vegetables and fruits do well and find a ready market, where the lowest freight rates by both rail and water prevail, coupled with the fact that good, rich prairie lands with plenty of timber can be had on favorable terms at from $5 to $8 per acre—and the reason is apparent why immigrants are now seeking the Coast Country of Texas in preference to any other spot in the Union. And they are coming on every excursion train of the Santa Fe Route; thousands are coming in annually. Those who come (I say it as a formerly northern man) are sure of a cordial southern welcome at all times to this bright land of sunshine and of flowers."

Under date of August 1, 1899, Mr. Slosson adds the following:

"During the Houston 'Fruit, Flower and Vegetable Festival,' held from December 5 to 11, 1898, Hon. Walter Whitney, Assistant Secretary of Agriculture, at Washington, D. C., attended the festival especially to note the progress made in the growing of Cuban tobacco, and to see the exhibits there displayed. To him it was a revelation of the capacity of the Coast Country soils, as the tobacco there shown equaled any raised in the United States, and brought on the market such prices as was supposed to be only paid for the best Havana tobacco. This only proves what has been said before—that our own people are not yet aware of the many possibilities awaiting development in this Coast Country of Texas."

Texas
As a Tobacco Growing State
● ● ●

Information for this article was prepared by Mr. A. R. Moore, President of the Texas Tobacco Growers' Association, of Houston, Texas. Mr. Moore says:

"Texas is now growing the highest grade of cigar tobacco in the United States, and many experts pronounce it equal to Cuban tobacco.

"The kind of tobacco that is being most successfully raised is the Vuelta Abajo, from Cuban seed. The growers are now experimenting in raising Sumatra wrapper, and from the samples submitted, there is no doubt but what we can grow as good grade of wrappers here as can the Island of Sumatra. The acreage in this state this year will be double that of last year, which will be about 10,000 acres.

"Hon. Milton Whitney, Chief Division of Soil of the Agriculture Department, who is also an expert on tobacco, said in an address at our last annual meeting, which was held in this city December 8th, 1898: 'Of the kinds of tobacco you growers are producing, that intended for the manufacture of cigars is the finest grown. From the samples of Texas tobacco I have seen, I am convinced that much of the Texas tobacco is quite similar to the best grade raised in Cuba.'

"The duty on Havana wrappers is $1.85 to $2.50 per pound and on fillers thirty-five to fifty cents, all of which can be saved the cigar manufacturer by using native stock, which is equally as good in every respect. Cigar wrappers and fillers grown in Southwestern Texas are equal in quality and flavor to the Cuban plant, a fact that manufacturers are beginning to realize. It needs no profound mathematician to figure out the value of home grown stock. With suitable soil, a salubrious climate, good markets and quick returns the tobacco planter is forging to the front and building up a fortune for himself.

"Read carefully the following testimonials, procured by Mr. Harrison of Harrison & Jones, Kansas City, a brother of ex-president Harrison:

By H. S. Edler "I am a tobacco raiser as well as cigar manufacturer; came from Illinois to Willis, in Montgomery County; have grown eight crops of cigar tobaccos in South Texas; was among the first to plant cigar tobacco in Montgomery County, Texas; have raised a crop of tobacco in Angelina County, Texas, this year, and for some of my cigar wrappers am offered $2 per pound. I have examined two samples of soil from a tract of 27,000 acres at Olive, Texas, in Hardin County, and I pronounce the samples shown me to be first-class cigar tobacco lands, both for wrappers and fillers, but more especially adapted to growing high grade cigar wrappers. I can cheerfully recommend these soils to anyone wishing to buy lands for the growing of high grade cigar stuff."

By John H. Twyman Of Wilson & Twyman, Kansas City, Mo., wholesale dealers in domestic and Key West cigars:

"I have had seven years' experience in the cigar business and feel that I am competent to judge of the quality of tobacco necessary to make a first-class cigar. I had the privilege some days ago of examining in your office some samples of cigar leaf tobacco raised in Southeastern Texas, and I unhesitatingly state that a great many of the samples examined I consider very fine and equal in every way to the finest Havana tobacco, the duty on which is $1.85 per pound."

By J. C. Mitchelson Of Mitchelson & Hibbard, Kansas City, Mo., dealers in leaf tobacco:

"It has been my privilege to examine Texas tobacco of different years' crops. I have also visited Southeastern Texas in the interests of our firm, to examine the soil in that section and the tobacco grown there. The cultivation of cigar tobacco has been my life-work, and it is a pleasure for me to be able to give my favorable opinion in regard to the soil and tobacco raised in Southeastern Texas. I visit all the different states where cigar tobacco is raised and visit Cuba annually in the interests of our firm. Some of the samples from Southeastern Texas are the nearest like the famous Vuelta Abajo from the Pinar del Rio district of western Cuba I have ever seen. Some of the Texas tobacco I consider equal in appearance to tobacco, the market price of which, in Pinar del Rio, has been $3 per pound for wrapper purposes. The soil in Southeastern Texas is the nearest like the soil in Cuba of any we have in our tobacco-producing states.

"The cost of fertilizing lands and preparing them to grow such high grades of tobacco in the northern states is from five to ten times the cost of our Texas lands, which have the necessary natural fertilizers and soils that can produce a much higher grade than can be raised there. Lands suitable for tobacco raising can be purchased here from $5 to $10, in tracts from fifty acres to 20,000 acres, either for individuals or colonization purposes.

"A stock company has been formed in Kansas City, Mo., for the purpose of owning and planting, this year, a tobacco farm of 1,000 acres near Olive, in this State.

"The demand for high grade tobacco is far in excess of the supply, and it will be years before the supply will be equal to the demand. Nine-tenths of the Texas tobacco is now being sold in Eastern markets as Cuban tobacco, at prices from $1 to $1.50 per pound.

"The half has not been told about the bright future and prospects for the tobacco culture of Texas. There is not a large section in the world which can produce as fine tobacco as we are raising here, and with our intelligent methods of handling staples of this kind, we will soon surpass any country in the world in producing high grade tobaccos.

"Judging by the antiquated manner in which the Cubans are handling their product Texas will soon take the lead in this industry. When we speak of Cuba as a tobacco growing country the natural inference is that all Cuba raises this high grade goods, but such is not the case. It is a little strip of country in the western part of Cuba, about 160 miles long by thirty miles wide, known as the Pinar del Rio province, wherein is located the celebrated Vuelta Abajo district. All nations of the earth are now using cigar tobacco from this district, and Cuba, in her most palmy days, was never able to supply the world with this famous tobacco. From the above information it is evident that, with our climatic conditions and soil, we will soon surpass Cuba."

Secretary Wilson's Views

• • •

Hon. James Wilson, Secretary of Agriculture, Washington, D. C., recently visited the Coast Country. In an interview he says:

"The Coast Country is immense. That expresses it in a word. But a most singular development appears here. You are preparing to handle the products of several states back of you, and yet, within an hour's ride you have thousands of acres of the finest land in the world—land that will raise anything —unsettled, unused, for sale at $15 per acre. I have never encountered such a condition anywhere else, for, as a rule, lands in the suburbs of the great cities are worth $150 to $400 an acre. Why it is so I do not know; but it is so. Within the past few years a few people have taken advantage of this opportunity. They have bought lands in this Coast Country, and they are making money—lots of it.

"The States back of Texas have been developed. The people have made money, and there are millions of dollars lying idle in the banks. This money will seek investment, and the people will take advantage of the opportunity to buy your splendid lands cheap and they will develop them. Texas is a splendid State—a great empire. It has started upon an era of development and progress. You know it has been said that during the late war the people of the United States have discovered themselves; they begin to appreciate what they have.

"I think that it is one of the finest countries in the world, and the more I see of it, the more I think so. I talked to the people awhile at Alvin. I saw some Iowa friends there. I can't understand how it is that such growing cities as Houston and Galveston can have such fine prairie between them and so much of it untilled. We want the people to get in on that and bring it into cultivation.

"My friends, this is a wonderful country. It seems to me you can raise anything here. Your soil is as good as our soil in Iowa. If I was a young man I'd pack my grip and come to Texas. The conditions and the prospects for development are such that I could not afford to remain away."

Real Estate Agents' Opinions

• • •

If it is your business to buy and sell coffee, you master every detail in order to know all there is worth knowing on the subject; to be an expert in grading and pricing. So it is with land. A reliable real estate agent can furnish more common sense facts about a farm than the owner himself—because the owner only knows about his own land, while it is the agent's business to be informed regarding all sorts of farms. One talks from the retail, the other from the wholesale point of view. Below are given extracts from interviews with three prominent Houston real estate agents, which recently appeared in a leading journal of that city:

By Mrs. Bettie Bryan "I can name at least a dozen counties in Southern and Southeastern Texas in which the waste lands would not amount to as much as 5 per cent of the total area, provided the country was supplied with a proper system of ditches and drainage. The great bulk of these lands are as fine for the production of all the cereals, cotton, fruit, berries, vegetables, in fact everything that grows in this climate, as can be found anywhere.

"The great variety of crops that can be grown makes the country very attractive to the agriculturist; but I am especially impressed with its possibilities as a rice producing section."

By C. W. Hahl "What do I think about the development of the agricultural resources of the Texas Coast Country? Why, this country is being improved so fast that our home people cannot keep up with the procession. Up to the past five or six years many crops which are now successfully and very profitably raised here were supposed to be a failure in this country. Northerners say that we have the finest country on earth (the Coast Country) and it will be the garden spot of the United States before many years; that our advantages are many and great over the Northern States in climate, markets, shipping facilities, cheap building material, saving in clothing, and by raising nearly everything one eats; that our stock runs out and feeds the year round, while they have to feed from six to seven months; and last, but not least, our cheap, good lands that are offered here from $5 to $10 per acre, are just as good and will raise as much as lands up north worth $40 to $80 per acre."

By J. H. Bright "Many years ago you could trade a two dollar and a half saddle pony for a section of Texas land, but you can't do it now. Why? Because there was one person (man, woman or child) to each 1,000 acres of land in this great State, and today there are almost 300 acres to each man, woman or child.

"Now everything is changed. The cattle interest has moved westward and the land owner has found new uses for his lands instead of grazing vast herds of long horns. He is making his lands bring him a bigger profit by cultivation, or by selling them to those who will cultivate them. In this way a new era has been inaugurated.

"We have practical demonstration that our coast lands will produce sugar, rice, corn, cotton, all sorts of grass, melons, vegetables, fruits and berries. You ask, how much do you make per acre? As an example we'll take corn, because everyone can compare corn. There are a great many reports on field averages of corn in the Coast Country that show 46 bushels is the average on lands that are properly tilled. There is a report on a farm in Brazoria county that shows an average of 57½ bushels on a field of twenty acres of sod land. Now this sod land is worth $10 to $15 per acre, but if you will stop to compare the value of products gathered from $10 or $15 lands against Kansas, Illinois, Tennessee or Kentucky $100 per acre lands, you will find that you can pay for your purchases of Coast Country lands with the products gathered the first year and have enough left over to keep your family and stock. Are such lands high?

"The Coast Country is a paradise for a poor man. He can pay for his farm and accumulate a larger domain while he is taking care of and raising a family to occupy it."

What One Man Has Done

• • •

In the *Saturday Review*, Galveston, April 16, 1898, appears an interesting article by Mr. Richard Spillane, entitled, "The Story of a Coast Country Experiment." It takes the form of an interview with Rev. J. J. Shirley, one of the pioneer fruit and vegetable growers at Alvin. Extracts from the most valuable portions appear below :

"How much land have you in cultivation?" I asked.

"I have," said Mr. Shirley, "something over 2,000 pear trees. Those trees you see there are the first I planted. Of the 2,000 in the orchard between 800 and 1,000 are now bearing. Year by year I have extended my orchard. The trees over there to the west are young. A few years more and they will bear. I have, all told, 44 or 45 acres in cultivation. Over there to the southwest I have peaches and plums. The big cabbage field you passed as you came up toward the gate is mine."

"What has been the result in a financial way from your farm and orchard?" I asked.

"I have not," said the reverend gentleman, "kept what you would call a set of books, so I can only answer in a general way. While my orchard has been growing, I have grown strawberries, corn, cotton, sweet and Irish potatoes, cabbage, okra, English peas, beets, turnips, radishes, celery, onions, vegetable musk, sugar cane, sorghum, squash, watermelons, canteloupes, red pepper, and dozens and dozens of other things in the rows between the fruit trees. Every month in the year I have been kept busy sowing and gathering some crop. You know we raise two or three crops a year here on the same land.

"When I came here, as I tell you, I had $485. Well, I have paid for my land and I have bought more land. I have spent $2,000 in improvements in the way of houses. I have raised my family. I have sent my sons to Georgetown University and had them educated. I sent my daughter to Granbury College. I've had money in bank."

"Have you had any offers for your farm?"

"Yes, many. I should think I've had one hundred or more. The largest amount offered was $16,000 cash."

"And you wouldn't sell?"

"No," was the clergyman's reply.

"Mr. Shirley," said I, "there has been a great deal of discussion about this fruit country between Houston and Galveston. Some men have failed; some have been successful. Will you tell me—you should be in a position to know—what is necessary for success?"

"Any man," said Mr. Shirley, "who is willing to work and who has a little money to back him up until he gets started can succeed. Brains—good common sense, I mean—muscle and money mean success in this Coast Country. There is more in the man than in the land. Some men are adapted by nature for fruit growing and for gardening. Some men have the power of adapting themselves to it. Some men would make a failure on any land. Any man who is at all practical can come into this Coast Country and, if he had enough money to carry him over the first two years, he ought to run along like a top after that."

"How much land should a man take?"

"I do not think a man should go over 30 acres. He shouldn't work more than 20 acres. He should have a little pasturage."

I asked the Rev. Mr. Shirley to tell me what had been the monetary return to him from the various crops he had raised.

"It's difficult for me to tell you exactly," he replied. "Take strawberries, for instance. Some years I grow a good many of them, two or three acres, maybe. Other years I grow only an acre. The crop and the price vary. I think it would be conservative to put the monetary return of strawberries at $250 an acre. They need a good deal of attention, you know.

"Snap beans; that is a good crop. They pay from $50 to $60 an acre. I raise them in the spring and after gathering the crop I put the land into cotton.

"Of cotton I raise a bale to the acre on open ground and half a bale to the acre when I plant it between the rows of fruit trees.

"Corn goes 20 bushels to the acre.

"Sweet and Irish potatoes I grow between the

rows in the orchards. Of Irish potatoes I raise from 50 to 75 bushels to the acre. Of sweet potatoes I raise 100 bushels.

"Cabbage is a winter crop. I plant in October and harvest in January, February and March. Last year my return from cabbage was $100 per acre.

"Okra grows magnificently in this country.

"English peas are particularly adapted to this soil and pay well. I make $100 an acre from the crop I sow.

"Beets do well, but I haven't grown many.

"Turnips are profitable. Rutabagas and spring turnips grow as well here as any place in the country.

"Radishes—they are simply prolific.

"Celery is destined to be one of our great crops, I believe. This is essentially a celery region and where proper attention is given the crop is as fine as anyone could desire.

"Onions require a great deal of care and when it is given we have excellent crops.

"I have experimented with rice, with vegetable musk, with sugar cane and with sorghum, and the result has been good. The yield from sugar cane has been 300 gallons to the acre. The sorghum is fine.

"It is needless, I presume, to tell you what a great region this is for squash, watermelons, and cantaloupes. To grow watermelons or cantaloupes no preparation is necessary further than to turn over the sod."

"Now," said I, "tell me about the pears, the peaches and the plums."

"I am growing two varieties of pears—the Keiffer and the Le Conte. Both are successful, but my orchard will not show as good returns as will those of other orchards in the Coast Country. My orchard, from the fact that it is the oldest in the Alvin district, has been the place to which visitors have made pilgrimages. Not only that, but, from the fact that it was the first to bear, my neighbors have come to me to examine the fruit. I have always allowed visitors or my neighbors to help themselves to fruit, so, you see, the yield will appear smaller than it really was. I think one-half of the crop each year has gone in the way I explained.

"The Le Conte trees begin to bear when six years old. The Keiffer bears when four. The first year my trees bore fruit they averaged—that is, I sold—one-half bushel of pears to the tree. I got $2.00 per bushel. The second year the trees bore, or, rather, I sold, at the rate of one bushel to the tree. This year I will sell about five bushels to the tree."

"How much do you get per bushel for pears?"

"I expect at the least $1.00 per bushel. Those I sell in small lots I believe will bring $1.50 per bushel. Those I ship will bring $1.00 per bushel."

"How about plums and peaches?"

"Peaches grow finely here, but the trees are short lived. After bearing three or four years the trees die out. The same applies to plums. Figs are profitable and easy to cultivate."

"Do you make use of such pears as you do not ship away?"

"Assuredly. I have made pear cider here that my neighbors buy and when I let the cider go to vinegar, I have no trouble selling it at 25 cents per gallon. I am about to build a cider press that will turn out three barrels a day. I am going into the vinegar making business, and have no doubt the worth of the article and the purity of the making will create a demand that will support the industry."

I asked Mr. Shirley if he thought there was any danger when all the pear trees in the Coast Country got to yielding that the market would be glutted.

"Gracious, no!" he replied. "Why, some gentlemen from London, who were here, and who were asked what they thought about it said the city of London could consume the entire fruit crop of this region.

"You see, we fruit growers have made a good many mistakes heretofore. We are only now learning our business after having been in the crucible of experience. Formerly we didn't know exactly the proper time to pick the fruit or exactly the way to ship it. Now we have our eyes open. We know something about cold storage, too. And we know where and when to ship."

"What have been the elements that have militated against the Coast Country?" Rev. Mr. Shirley was asked.

"Drainage has been one of the great drawbacks," he replied. "That we are overcoming slowly, but surely. Irrigation is another. It will not be many years before we have these problems solved. Everything we do is for improvement; every season we are nearer to success.

Other Texas Counties

• • •

Below is given a very brief resume of the various Texas counties traversed by the Gulf, Colorado & Santa Fe Railway, excepting those near the Gulf coast which are fully described elsewhere.

In view of the general plan of the pamphlet, which is to call special attention to the Gulf coast section, a complete "write-up" cannot be furnished here. But even this condensation may convey some idea of the immense resources of inland Texas, an empire in wealth and power and possibilities.

Austin County Population 20,000; county seat, Bellville, population 1,500. Well watered by Brazos River, also Mill Creek, East Bernal and other creeks. Along Brazos River and Mill Creek are forests of oak, ash, elm and black walnut; fire-wood abundant everywhere. Area of Austin County, 700 square miles; one-third under cultivation and two-thirds fenced. Soil is a black, sandy loam in the river bottoms; a black, sticky quality on the prairies and one-third sandy black in hills. Principal crop, cotton; corn and oats also raised and every variety of vegetables. Population mainly a prosperous class of Germans. Best of educational advantages. Summers are never oppressive, while winters are short and mild. Cyclones have never visited this section, and a total failure of crops is unknown.

Bell County Population about 50,000; county seat, Belton, population 5,000. Well watered with four rivers, numerous creeks and springs; also many fine artesian wells in and around Belton. Timbered with oak, pecan, cedar, etc. Gold and silver found in small quantities in the hills. Area of the county, 1,045 square miles, two-thirds under cultivation. Soil is of a black-waxy nature; about one-third timber land mixed with sandy gravel. Principal crops are cotton, corn, oats, wheat, hay and sugar cane. Various industries: flouring mills, cotton and oil mills, cotton gins, compresses, canning factories, stone quarries and brick yards. One of the most fertile and wealthiest counties in Texas. Plenty of cheap lands from $3 to $20 per acre. The abundance of cotton and wool at Belton affords a fine opening there for cotton and woolen manufacturing. Pleasant winter and summer climate. Never colder than 20° above zero in winter.

Bosque County Population about 18,000; county seat, Meridian, population 1,500. Well watered by Bosque and Brazos Rivers, Steel's, Spring and Meridian Creeks. Artesian water easily obtained anywhere from 500 to 900 feet. Fuel and fence posts can be had from the timbered land. Soil is a black-waxy quality, except on the rivers where it is sandy. Principal crops are cotton, corn, wheat, oats, rye, barley, millet and sorghum; also all kinds of fruits are raised. The residents are a prosperous class of people. Hot summers, but always a cool breeze; mild winters, very little snow and ice. Land is cheap.

Brown County Population 17,000; county seat, Brownwood, population 5,200. Watered by Colorado River, Pecan, Bayou, Jim and Ned Creeks. Land well timbered. Area of county, 1,100 square miles. Two hundred thousand acres under cultivation. Soil, a chocolate loam. Crops consist of cotton, corn, wheat, oats, sorghum, millet, fruits and vegetables. Farmers and merchants are prosperous. Very temperate climate all the year round. Rich, productive lands at $4 to $6 per acre on easy terms.

Burleson County Population 15,000; county seat, Caldwell, population 1,500. Land is watered by Brazos and Yegua Rivers and Second Creek. Plenty of timber. Area of the county, 1,000 square miles, about one-third under cultivation. Soil, sandy black. Principal crop is cotton. Summers hot, winters cool and damp.

Coleman County Population 7,000; county seat, Coleman, population 2,800. Well watered by Colorado River, Center, Hords, Jim, Ned, North, Pecan and Bayou Creeks. Plenty of timber for fuel, also large coal deposits in southern part of county. Area of Coleman County, 1,290 square miles; one-sixteenth of it under cultivation. Black prairie land; sandy soil in parts of the county. Principal crops: cotton, wheat, oats and all small grains. Cattle, horses and mules are raised in large numbers. Gulf breeze makes the summers cool, while winters are delightful. Climate cannot be excelled for healthfulness. Lands are cheap; county is being rapidly settled. Schools and churches located in every part.

Collin County Population about 35,000; county seat, McKinney, population 6,000. Land watered by numerous creeks. Large quantities of Osage orange, oak and hemlock timber. Area of county, 30 square miles, four-fifths under cultivation. Black-waxy soil. Crops consist of corn, cotton, wheat and oats; stock-raising is also followed. Principal industries are cotton and oil mills. County thickly settled by thrifty, law-abiding, prosperous farmers. Churches and school-houses in every community. Land in cultivation sells from $20 to $30 per acre. Summers are warm, average temperature 96°; winters mild and pleasant, seldom any snow or ice.

Cook County Population 40,000; county seat, Gainesville, population 11,500. Watered by Red River, Trinity and Clear Creeks, and other streams. One-half the county is timbered land. Area, 933 square miles. Soil is black-waxy, sandy and red sandy. Principal crops: corn, wheat and cotton. The citizens are prosperous. Gainesville, the county seat, situated on the Trinity River, is a busy city; has eleven churches, six brick school houses, two flouring mills, an ice factory, an iron foundry, a cotton compress, a broom factory, soap factory, cotton seed oil mills, pressed brick works, four newspapers, three banks. The Santa Fe Railway shops are located here.

Dallas County Population 90,000; county seat, Dallas, population 64,224. Well watered by Trinity River and three tributaries, also small creeks. Plenty of timber, building stone and fire and pottery clay. Area of county, 900 square miles. About 165,000 acres under cultivation, or seventy per cent. of tillable land. Soil of all varieties from sandy to heavy black-waxy. Principal crops: cotton, corn, wheat and oats. Market-gardening and fruit-raising have developed to great extent; also profitable dairy and stock industries. Dallas is largest manufacturing city in state of Texas. The settlers are industrious and prosperous. Climate mild both summer and winter. Farming lands for sale at moderate prices. Unusual opportunities for manufacturing industries.

Delta County Population 12,500; county seat, Cooper, population 2,000. Plenty of hardwood timber. Area of county, 290 square miles. Eight hundred small farms in Delta County. Soil, black and very rich, from four to fifteen feet deep. Crops: corn, cotton and alfalfa. Farmers and merchants prosperous. Winters mild, summers warm and dry. Land can be rented for from $4 to $5 per acre, and bought for from $20 to $30 per acre.

Denton County Population 40,000; county seat, Denton, population 5,000. Well watered; artesian water can be obtained at from 300 to 400 feet. Timber in the eastern part of the county. Area of Denton County, 900 square miles; about 100 square miles under cultivation. Soil sandy and mixed with black land. Principal crops are wheat, oats, corn and cotton. Finest wheat belt in Texas extends from Denton west; is about twenty miles wide, and this year averaged between twenty and twenty-five bushels per acre; stock raising and shipping is carried on to considerable extent. The settlers are a thrifty, prosperous people. Mild summers and pleasant winters.

Ellis County Population 65,000; county seat, Waxahachie, population 7,000. Land watered by Trinity River and artesian wells. Along the streams there is timber sufficient for fuel. Area of county, 950 square miles, three-fourths under cultivation. Soil is a black-waxy quality. General crops: hay, corn, oats, wheat and cotton. Farmers are prosperous. Climate, mild.

Fannin County Population 60,000; county seat, Bonham, population 5,000. Watered by Red River, its tributaries and springs. Plenty of timber along water courses. Area of county, 1,089 square miles, half in cultivation. Soil, black and waxy; along the river it is

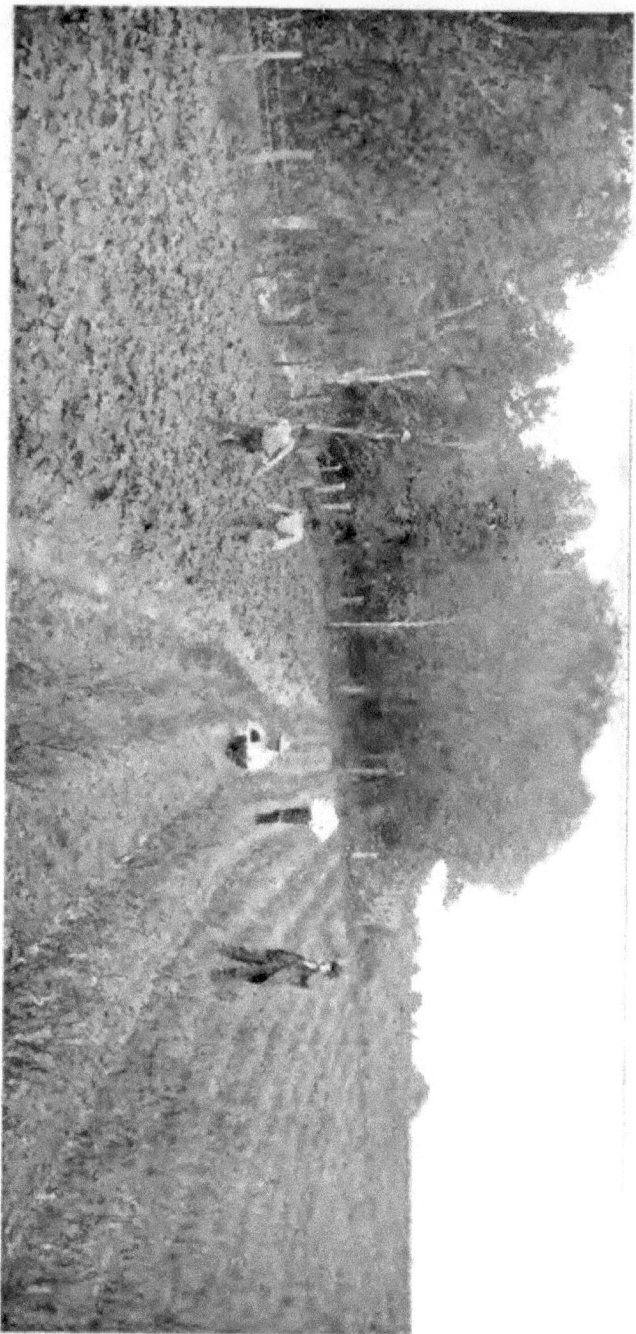

STRAWBERRIES OR ONIONS—TAKE YOUR CHOICE

sandy. Crops are cotton, corn, oats, hay, wheat and garden products of all kinds. Settlers are unusually prosperous. Climate is mild, averaging from 68° to 75°. Fannin County is noted for the quality of her cotton, which frequently sells for higher price than that of adjacent counties.

Grimes County Population 25,000; county seat, Anderson, population 500. Is watered by Brazos and Navasota Rivers and their tributaries. Timber and minerals are found in parts of the county. Area is 781 square miles, one-half being timbered and the remainder prairie land; 100,000 acres under cultivation. Sandy and black waxy soil. Principal crops: cotton, cane and corn. Mild climate, average summer temperature 95°; winter 60°. Lands are cheap; a good county for investors and home-seekers.

Hunt County Population 40,000; county seat, Greenville, population 7,500. Well watered by tanks and cisterns; abundant timber. Soil, black-waxy and sandy. Principal crops: corn, cotton, grains, hay, fruits and vegetables. Cattle and hogs are raised. Farmers and merchants are prosperous. Climate mild in winter, and south breeze makes the summers pleasant. Plenty of good, cheap land from $10 to $30 per acre.

Johnson County Population 19,000; county seat, Cleburne, population 7,500. Watered by various streams and artesian wells; abundance of timber. Area of county, 1,600 square miles; twenty-five per cent. under cultivation. Soil, black-waxy and sandy loam. Principal products consist of cotton, wheat, oats, corn, and cattle. The settlers are prosperous. Pleasant climate the year round, especially in the winter. Land can be bought on easy terms; light taxation, good schools and ready market for farm products.

Lampasas County Population 7,565; county seat, Lampasas, population 2,500. Watered by Lampasas and Colorado Rivers, numerous creeks and springs. Plenty of cedar and other fuel timber, also valuable pecan timber. Area of county, 858 square miles; about 50,000 acres in cultivation. A portion of the soil first class for farming, some is sandy and clay. Principal crops are cotton and grains. Industries, wool growing and sheep and cattle raising. Residents a very prosperous people. Excellent climate the year round. Fine school facilities; good homes are cheap. Largest sulphur springs in the world are here.

Lamar County

Population 37,302; county seat, Paris, population 15,000. Watered by Red and North Sulphur Rivers, Pine and Saunders Creeks, and other small streams. Water for stock and domestic purposes easily obtained at average depth of 50 feet. Timber abundant along water courses, such as hackberry, elm, ash, oak and hickory, of splendid quality; also pecan and other varieties, including the famous *bois d'arc*. Soil mostly a rich alluvial and black-waxy land, all exceedingly fertile. Principal crops: cotton, wheat, oats, barley, rye, millet, sugar-cane, garden vegetables, also all kinds of fruits. Stock raising is profitable. Exceedingly fine climate; the nights, visited by soft breezes tempered by Gulf winds, are always cool. Area of Lamar County is 900 square miles; most of the land under cultivation. Excellent school houses and comfortable churches.

McLennan County

Population 50,000; county seat, Waco, population 25,000. Watered by Brazos, Bosque, Aquilla and other rivers, also numerous creeks and wells. Timber is abundant; oil is also being developed. Area of the county, 1,083 square miles; half under cultivation. Soil of river lands, sandy loam; prairie lands, mostly black-waxy. Principal crops: cotton, corn, wheat, oats and all vegetables; also berries and fruits of every variety. Farmers and merchants are generally very prosperous. Climate is pleasant, being tempered both winter and summer by Gulf breezes; average temperature for past ten years, 69°. Good homes at reasonable prices.

Milam County

Population 32,000; county seat, Cameron, population 5,000. Land watered by Little River, Brazos River, San Gabriel, Elm and Pond Creeks. Plenty of post oak timber, also fine lignite beds. Area of Milam County, 11,000 square miles; 75,000 acres under cultivation. Soil, black-waxy and gray post oak with clay sub-soil. Crops consist of cotton, corn and oats. Principal industries are oil mill, compress, water works, electric light and ice plants. Both summer and winter pleasant and healthful. Good land, excellent social advantages and fine schools.

Mills County Population 7,500; county seat, Goldthwaite, population 1,875. Watered by Colorado River, Pecan, Bayou, Bennett, Brown, Lampasas, Miller and Bull's Creeks. Well water can be obtained at from 25 to 100 feet. Half the county well timbered. There is iron ore and traces of silver and coal. Area of the county, 720 square miles; about one-fifth under cultivation. Soil, mixed, sandy and black-waxy. Crops are cotton, corn, wheat, oats, sorghum, millet, potatoes, melons and vegetables; also small fruits. Farmers are doing well and no financial failures among merchants. Climate delightful the year round. A great health resort. An excellent place for those afflicted with pulmonary troubles; no chills or fevers. Lands may be bought at low prices. Good schools and churches in every section of the county.

Montgomery County Population 13,000; county seat, Conroe, population 600. Watered by numerous running streams. Plenty of timber of all kinds. Deposits of iron not yet developed. Area of county 1,150 square miles; about one-fourth under cultivation. Soil, principally black-waxy and sandy. Best crops are sugar-cane, corn, cotton, potatoes and tobacco; also fruits. Farmers and merchants prosperous. Summer climate with average temperature of 75° and winter 40°. Good lands, exceedingly cheap, on easy terms.

Parker County Population 30,000; county seat, Weatherford, population 7,000. Well watered by running streams, springs and wells. Plenty of timber and coal. Area of Parker County is 900 square miles; about 125,000 acres under cultivation. Soil, partly sandy loam, black-waxy and black-waxy loam. Crops are cotton, corn, wheat, oats, hay, vegetables and fruits of all kinds. Climate mild in summer (Gulf breeze), variable in winter.

IN A SWEET POTATO FIELD.

Runnels County Population 4,000; county seat, Ballinger, population 1,800. Watered by Colorado River and several creeks. Some timber and building stone. Area of county is 900 square miles; about one-fifth under cultivation. Soil, a sandy loam. Principal crops are melons, corn, wheat, oats and cotton. Stock-raising is the leading industry. Climate warm in summer with pleasant breeze; winters agreeable.

Tarrant County Population 60,000; county seat, Ft. Worth, population 25,000. Watered by Trinity River and branches; also creeks. About one-fourth of the county well timbered; half under cultivation; one-fourth grazing land. Soil, sandy and black-waxy land. Principal crops: corn, wheat, oats, cotton and all kinds of vegetables and fruits; also pecans. Delightful breezes in summer; winters warm and considerable rain. Good schools and churches. Population is progressive and liberal. Good opportunities to make money by stock-raising.

Tom Green County Population 7,500; county seat, San Angelo, population 4,000. Watered by Concho River and Spring and Dove Creeks; some timber. Area, 1,800 square miles. Soil, a sandy loam. Principal crops: cotton, milo, maize and sorghum; also hay. Warm, dry summers; winters dry and very little freezing weather. Farmers are prosperous. A good country for stock farmers and farming by irrigation.

Washington County Population 30,000; county seat, Brenham, population 8,000. Watered by Brazos River and Yegua, Jackson, New Years and Mill Creeks. One-third timber land, some minerals. Area of county, 600 square miles; 75 per cent. under cultivation. Soil very rich, black-waxy, black, sandy and loam. Crops, cotton and corn. Manufacturing is the principal industry. Climate, mild; average temperature in summer 80°, in winter 38°. A total failure of crops is unknown.

Index
••

MAP OF
TEXAS COAST
COUNTRY.

COLORADO   K   A

Conejos   Trinidad   Liberal

Antonito

Vasquez

Mineral City

Optima   Beaver

Dillon

Espanola   Greenville   Texline   Hansford   W

SANTA FE   Hot Springs   Higgins

Las Vegas   Tascosa   Mendota

Lamy   R.   Mobeetie

N E W   Canadian   Amarillo   Panhandle

Puerto de Luna   La Plata   Claude   Wellingt

Hereford   FT.   Red

Fort Sumner   Texico   Tulia   Memphis

Surry Side   Plainview   Childress

White Oaks   Kenna   Paducah

Lubbock   Emma   Rayner

M E X I C O   L L A N O

Lincoln   Roswell   E S T A C A D O

Rio   Hondo

Lower Penasco   Robbing Range   Gail   Snyder   A

Rio   Penasco   Carlsbad   Sweetwater   TEXAS

Concho

Anthony   Malaga   Big Spring

El Paso   Riverton   Douro   Midland   Robert

TEXAS   Pecos   Sterling City   GULF

PAC.   Pecos   River   SAN ANGELO

Ciudad Juarez   Toyah   Sherwood

Sierra Blanca   Ft. Stockton   E

RIO   Dalberg   Ft. Lancaster   Ozona   Ma

T   Valentine   Junction City

Pilares   Fort Davis   Freder

S. P. CO.   Alpine   Rock Springs

Carrizo   Marfa   Pecan Spring   Kerrvill

GRANDE   Shafter   Sanderson   Shumla

Vado de Piedras   NORTE   B

M   Presidio   Del Rio   Spofford J

E   Presidio del Norte   Presidio San Vicente   Un   Sa

Conchos   DEL

X   Sto. Domingo   Ciudad Porfirio Diaz   Eagle Pa

I   Canon de Encinillas   R. Sabinas   C

R.   Julimes   El Zacate   Sabinas   Felipe   San

Rand, McNally & Co., Engravers, Chicago.

BETWEEN
CHICAGO, ST. LOUIS
AND TEXAS.